Armor

Sean Morrison

Armor

Illustrated by the Author

Thomas Y. Crowell Company / New York

To Francis Grace,

To Whom It Was Promised

Laus Deo Semper

An Introduction

The story of armor is really a story of people—the people who made it and the people who wore it. We can tell quite a lot about people from the armor they wore: by how much they wore, how skillfully it was made, and who wore it.

Unfortunately, in telling the story of armor, we have to do some guessing. Very little armor of the period before A.D. 1400 remains. Iron rusts away; bronze and copper corrode. Armor is buried in a lost grave with the man who wore it. Pieces lie on battlefields covered over by the passing of years. Very few writers bothered to write about the armor of their time. To them, it was such an everyday thing that it was not worth mentioning. Much of what we know comes from paintings, illustrations in books, wall carvings, and statues. We also have other objects made at the same time which tell us what materials were used then and how skilled the craftsmen were. Weapons from nearly every age have been found, which can give us more clues about what armor was worn.

There are still many mysteries. Who invented mail? Why did the Greeks never change their armor while their arts and crafts advanced by leaps and bounds? Who invented gunpowder, which put an end to armor, and who invented the first gun?

The story of armor is an adventure story. It is a mystery story too. But then, that is half the fun.

I am indebted to the staff of the John Woodman Higgins Armory in Worcester, Massachusetts; to Allen D. Wassall, Director, for his interest and enthusiasm, and to Albert Gagne, Curator, and his assistant, Ebenezer Bauchop, two fine craftsmen in the armorers' tradition, for their expert advice. This magnificent collection is too little known and should not be missed by anyone interested in armor.

My thanks go also to Miss Francena Harris of the Pierpont Morgan Library in New York for help with the material on which the jacket design is based; to Graham Webster of the University of Birmingham, England, for putting me straight on the lorica segmentata; and to my wife, who, in retrospect, seems to have written most of the book, and who kept the children out of my hair while I staggered through the rest of it.

Contents

ONE | *The Beginnings* 1

TWO | *The Classical World—Greece* 33

THREE | *The Classical World—Rome* 51

FOUR | *The Age of Mail* 99

FIVE | *The Age of Change* 129

SIX | *The Age of Plate* 171

SEVEN | *The Tournament* 221

EIGHT | *The New Age of Armor* 249

Index 253

Hittite Charioteer

1
The Beginnings

The early history of civilized man is a tale of war. Nations rose out of nowhere, ruled, and crashed in ruins to be replaced by other nations who went through the same thing and were replaced in their turn. Races, tribes, and groups of people wandered in and out of the Middle East tangling things up even more. Sometimes the reason why things happened is not very clear. Even historians cannot agree about them. Sometimes they do not even agree about when they happened, which makes matters all the more difficult for the rest of us.

The history of the great nations of the Ancient World has been written many times before. We are going to look at only four of them: the Sumerians because they invented the phalanx and the chariot; the Hittites because they were the first to use the chariot for war; the Egyptians because they had the first professional army; and the Assyrians because they were the first to use iron for war, and because their heavily armored army was the best of the Ancient World.

Not many of the early nations wore armor. For one thing, the Middle East, where they lived, is too hot. Even the lightest kinds of armor, made of padded cloth or leather, were too much. Metal armor was even heavier and metal becomes hot enough to burn skin under the hot sun.

Metal armor was rare in the Ancient World for another reason. Most metals, at that time, were hard to find and very expensive. Only kings and noblemen could afford weapons and armor of metal. Iron was little used, even though it is a common metal, because the early smiths did not have furnaces hot enough to melt it. They could melt copper and bronze, which is a mixture of copper and tin, and shape them by pouring them into molds. Iron had to be shaped by hammering. It even had to be taken out of the ore by hammering. Even then, the smith was left with just a few small beads of iron, which had to be hammered together to make a lump big enough to work with. All this took too much time and made iron very costly. It was so valuable that it was worth five times as much as gold.

Finally, most of the ancient peoples were archers, and archers like to keep their bodies and limbs free. The bow

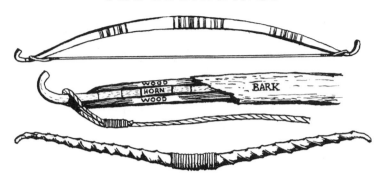

that they used was a composite bow, made of layers of horn glued between two layers of wood. It had been invented, probably, by the Semites who came out of the Arabian desert and spread through the Middle East and along the northern coast of Africa. To use a powerful bow like the composite bow, the bowman must be able to move and turn and bend easily. Armor makes this difficult, either because it is stiff or because it is heavy. So, many of the ancient races did without armor and looked to their bows to protect them.

The first civilized people were the Sumerians. We do not know where they came from, but by 4000 B.C. they were living in the rich lands between the Tigris and the Euphrates. They were a warlike people and great inventors. Among other things, they invented the phalanx and, about 3000 B.C., the chariot.

The phalanx is a battleline made up of several ranks of men standing shoulder to shoulder, one rank behind the other. They must be trained to move together, so that there are no gaps for the enemy to break into and so that the whole phalanx hits the enemy at once. (This is where the word *phalanx* comes from—the Greek *phalagx*, a club.) The phalanx was probably the best way for foot soldiers to fight, in the early days of hand-to-hand fighting. It was good for attack because it delivered a solid blow, and it was good in defense because there was always a new line of men waiting to fight if the front line was broken up or killed. Some kind of phalanx was used by every trained infantry army until the Middle Ages.

The Sumerians must have had a highly trained army to use the phalanx. This was very rare in early times. In fact, until the Age of Gunpowder, which began about A.D. 1500, most armies were made up of ordinary citizens who were called out when the king or one of the noblemen needed them. They were not trained as soldiers. They were not usually paid to fight. They even had to find their own weapons and armor. Since most of them were farmers, they could only go to war after the crops had been sown in the spring, and they had to be back in time for the harvest. This meant that wars were usually fought during the summer. Besides, the armies could only move when the roads were good. They had to travel on foot, or at best on horseback, carrying their supplies with them. This made the second Sumerian invention, the chariot, an important military item, too.

The Sumerian chariot was a clumsy cart. It was used to carry men and supplies, but it was too slow to take part in the fighting. At first it had four thick wooden

wheels. Later it was given two large wheels, which made it easier to steer. The floor was a thick block of wood, and the sides were made of leather stretched over a wooden frame. The front was higher than the driver's head. It was pierced with an eyehole and a hole for the reins. The chariot was pulled by a team of four wild asses harnessed to a long pole called the yoke pole. The Sumerians used asses because the horse had not yet arrived in the Middle East. When it did, the chariot became a weapon of war.

The Sumerian army was a citizen army of foot soldiers, led into battle by the king. They fought in a phalanx six ranks deep. It was probably the phalanx that made them the rulers of Mesopotamia. They wore very little armor. In fact, they wore very little of anything. The ordinary dress for a man was a long kilt and nothing else. The soldiers added an ankle-length cloak, covered with small

metal studs. They also wore copper helmets with pointed headpieces. The king's helmet was made of gold, hammered into curls and waves like his hair.

The phalanx carried huge rectangular shields, probably made of leather on a frame of wood. They stretched from a man's nose to his feet. The Sumerians' weapons were short spears and axes with copper heads. They did not have swords or bows. They knew nothing about bows until they were overwhelmed by the archers of Akkad in the twenty-second century B.C. By then, of course, it was too late to do anything about it.

With the defeat of the Sumerians, the first Age of Infantry came to a close. The chariot became the weapon of the first Age of Cavalry.

The new chariot was completely different from the heavy two- and four-wheeled carts of the Sumerians. It was drawn by horses, which had been brought into the Middle East by a wandering Indo-Germanic people called the Hurrians. Around 2000 B.C., the Hurrians had settled to the north of Syria, not far from the country of the Hittites. Somewhere in this region, the war chariot was invented, perhaps by the Hurrians, perhaps by the Hittites themselves. (The first book on horse training was written for a Hittite king in the fourteenth century B.C. by a Hurrian named Kikkuli.)

The war chariot had a light body made of a wooden frame covered with wicker, leather, or wooden panels. These were the sides, which were usually as high as the driver's waist. They ran almost all the way round the body of the chariot, leaving an opening at the back. The floor was made of wide leather strips, woven across one another, which worked like the springs of a car to soften the bumps.

The horses were harnessed to a yoke pole. It ran underneath the body and fitted into a slot in the back of the frame. The front of the frame was tied to the pole

with leather straps. The axle of the chariot ran underneath the yoke pole and was fastened to each side of the frame with leather thongs. The wheels, which turned on the axle, were held in place by pins. They were much larger than the Sumerian wheels, and made the chariot steadier. They were made of wood with metal or leather tires. Usually they had six spokes. Because they were so light, they "gave" whenever they hit a bump. This saved the charioteer from having his teeth rattled every time the chariot went over a small stone.

The chariot was drawn by a team of two or four horses, and carried two or three men. It completely changed warfare, and for a thousand years it ruled the battlefield.

The greatest charioteers were the Hittites. They were an Indo-Germanic people who arrived in Asia Minor about 2000 B.C. They took their name from the place where they first settled, Hatti-land.

For the first five centuries after they arrived, they were busy building up a commonwealth of tribes living in Asia Minor. They never had an empire in the way that Egypt or Assyria did. They made allies and friends, instead of slaves. In the Hittite "Empire," there were eight different languages, four different ways of writing them, and, one Egyptian scribe said, a thousand gods.

The Hittite army was a force of fast-moving chariots, who always tried to catch their enemies in the open and ambush them. They soon became the most feared warriors in the Middle East. The chariot was still a strange sight to most of their enemies. It must have scared the wits out of infantrymen, especially, to see a rank of chariots thundering down on them. Those that were not shot down were crushed beneath the flying hoofs and iron-rimmed wheels. Even if the horses were brought down, they crushed men as they fell.

The Hittite chariots carried three men, a driver and two archers. Most chariots carried only one fighting man, so the Hittites always had twice as many men for the hand-to-hand fighting that broke out when the chariots hit the enemy line. The archers carried two quivers of extra arrows fastened to the side of the chariot. Besides their bows, they had long, curved slashing swords. They carried short bronze shields, shaped like dumbbells. Beyond this, they had no armor at all. They moved too fast to need it, and, like all archers, preferred to keep their arms as free as possible.

There were also foot soldiers in the Hittite army, but they took little part in the battles. They guarded the baggage train and the camp, manned fortresses, and protected the king on the battlefield. Unlike most other kings at that time, the Hittite king considered himself too valuable to go dashing headfirst into the fighting. (The Hittites were famous for their sound good sense.)

The infantry had tall bronze helmets, which curved in at the top to a point. Large, rounded earflaps hung down from each side, and the neck was protected by a close-fitting neckguard which turned out sharply at the bottom. The crest of the helmet was probably made of horsehair. It ran over the top and turned into a long plume hanging down the back.

They carried huge, round shields, probably made of wood, which were held by a single metal loop at the back. They wore short tunics, or simply kilts, held at the waist by a wide leather belt. Their weapons were a very long spear, a long, straight sword, and a short battle-axe. The blade of the axe was sometimes shaped like a human hand, with the fingers grasping the shaft.

In the fourteenth century B.C., the Hittites marched south into Syria with the idea of adding it to their empire. Here they clashed with the Egyptians, who were moving north with the same idea in mind. The two great civilizations began a war that went on for two hundred years. It ended by destroying them both.

The Egyptians were one of the oldest civilized nations, but they had kept quietly to themselves. Their wars were mostly civil wars and they did very little fighting outside their own borders. In fact, they looked down on soldiers. They spent their time farming and helping to build pyramids.

For centuries, the only army they had in peacetime was the Pharaoh's bodyguard. There were also temple guards who protected the miners on the way to and from the quarries. In wartime, every citizen armed himself and turned out, but as soon as the fighting was over they went back quietly to farming and building pyramids.

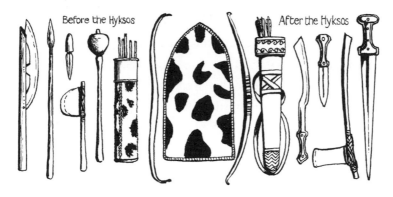

Their weapons were short spears, axes with copper blades tied to the shaft, stone-headed maces, and weak wooden bows. Their arrows were made of hardwood sharpened and hardened in a fire, or of reed shafts with flint heads. They had no swords. They had to use copper instead of bronze, because tin was scarce in Egypt.

They had rectangular shields made of bull's hide stretched over a wooden frame. Nothing more was needed against such weak weapons. For the same reason, they had no armor, although they let their hair grow into a thick mop to protect themselves from a rap on the head.

The old Egypt came to an end in the eighteenth century B.C. Egypt was overrun by a people called the Hyksos, which means Kings of the Barbarians. No one really knows who they were or where they came from. The most likely explanation is that they were Hurrians, driven south by the Hittites. Whoever they were, the Hyksos set up their own Pharaohs and ruled Egypt for over two hundred years.

During the time of the Hyksos, the Egyptians learned to use the chariot, the layered bow, and the sword. They learned to use bronze for sword blades, spears, axes, and arrowheads. They also learned to hate the Hyksos and all Asian peoples through them. In 1580 B.C., an Egyptian prince of Thebes, called Ahmose, raised a rebellion against the Hyksos and threw them out of Egypt. Ahmose became Pharaoh and was followed by many more warrior-rulers.

The Egyptians had changed. Driven to take up arms in order to free themselves, they had turned themselves into a military people. After the Hyksos were beaten, they did not go back to their old, more peaceful ways. They began to build an empire and to revenge themselves on the Asians. First, they took Libya and the Sudan with their rich gold mines. Then, they turned on Palestine and Syria. By the middle of the fifteenth century B.C., the Egyptian Empire stretched as far as the Euphrates.

The new Egyptian army was well armed and highly trained. It was made up of chariots and infantry. Most of the infantry and all the charioteers were archers. The rest were spearmen, swordsmen, and slingers.

The chariots were lighter and smaller than Hittite chariots, and carried only one archer and a driver. The sides of the body were made of thin wooden panels covered with molded stucco, a kind of white clay, and gaily painted. The Pharaoh's chariot was covered with sheets of electrum, a mixture of gold and silver. Every chariot

had two quivers of spare arrows fastened to the body, and a large leather bowcase with a spare bow in front. In peacetime, the chariots were kept in the royal stables, under guard, because they were so valuable.

The charioteers were all noblemen. Even so, they had to be able to repair their own chariots. They were taught how to take them to pieces and put them back together again. They also learned to handle horses, and to care for them. These noblemen of the new Egypt were professional soldiers. They had been made noblemen by the Pharaoh for their help in the rebellion against the Hyksos. Now they were the most powerful men in Egypt. Nobody despised the soldier any more.

The Pharaoh and the noblemen began to wear armor. They had two types of scale tunic. One was an ordinary tunic, with short sleeves; the other ran from the armpits to the hips and was held up by straps over the shoulders. The scales were made of bronze or hard Egyptian copper. They were usually shaped like leaves with a thick rib running down the middle. Sometimes, a gold or silver chest plate was worn with the short tunic. It was usually oval or crescent-shaped and hung round the neck on a heavy chain.

The Pharaoh wore a helmet called the war crown. It was made of stiff leather covered with small metal rings.

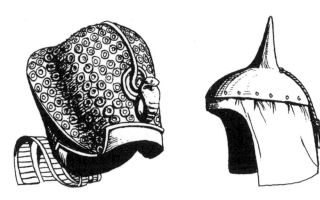

The top was round and bulged out like the head of the bishop in a chess set. Running down each side was a stiff flap, shaped like a fin. The bottom of the helmet was strengthened with thin metal bands, and the symbol of Egypt, the sacred cobra, was fastened to the front.

The noblemen had a helmet shaped like a rounded pouring funnel upside down. It had a curtain of leather or heavy cloth hanging down from the rim to the shoulders, to cover the sides and back of the neck.

The infantry was a mixture of Egyptians, Libyans, Nubians, Philistines, Sherden, and a dozen other tribes. Most of them came from the countries of the empire. Some were prisoners who had won their freedom by joining the army. Others had joined for the plunder, with which the mercenaries were paid. The best troops were the Libyan and Nubian archers, who were still famous for their skill in Roman times, and the Sherden swordsmen. The Sherden were a race of pirates from the Aegean Sea. They formed the Pharaoh's bodyguard, so they must have been crack troops.

Egyptian boys were sent to special schools, where they learned to handle bow, spear, sword, and shield. They ran, jumped, and wrestled to keep fit. The army was trained hard, too. They practiced marching in regiments. They had weapons drill and war games. In peacetime, the mercenary soldiers were sent to live and work on farms so that they would not get soft with easy living.

The archers were taught to fire all together in volleys. This was an Egyptian idea, and, in a way, it was as important as the invention of the phalanx. It made the Egyptian archers the most powerful infantry of their time. They could even tackle a line of chariots. Long after Egypt's might was gone, her archers were famous. They helped the Romans to build their empire in the first century A.D. They used the layered bow, as the noblemen did. They carried a bowcase on their back and a quiver on the belt, along with a leather pouch which held spare bow strings, oil for the bowstave and a sharpening stone.

The spearman carried a short stabbing spear with a bronze blade, and an axe or a khepesh. The khepesh was the Hyksos sword. It was a slashing weapon with a short curved blade like a sickle. The Sherden swordsman had a long stabbing sword and sometimes used a spear as well.

Most of the infantry wore some kind of armor and carried shields. The ordinary Egyptian shield was a rectangle with a rounded top. It had a round peephole near the top. It was made of wood about one inch thick and the front was painted to look like bull's hide. The Sherden had a different kind of shield. It was large and round, and the front was covered with metal studs.

The infantry armor was a heavily padded wool or linen tunic. It was stuffed with wool, which was sewn into place. Sometimes rows of small metal studs were added to strengthen the cloth. The tunic ran down to the knees but the skirt was split in several places, so the soldiers could move their legs freely. The cloth of the tunic was often dyed bright red or green or blue.

The Sherden had a short tunic with shoulder straps, like the nobleman's. It seems to have been made of strips of stiff leather, riveted to the cloth underneath. The stomach was protected by a long padded flap, hanging from the bottom of the tunic down to the knees. The Sherden also had metal helmets, which were rare in the Egyptian army. These were shaped like shallow bowls. They had a crest made of a thin rod with a ring on the end of it. Two small horns curved up from the bottom of the rod so that the whole thing looked like an anchor.

The rest of the infantry wore padded linen helmets or simple leather caps. The helmets had the same shape as their hair style, a rounded top with long sides falling straight to the shoulders. The leather caps fitted close to the head, with a bite-shaped piece cut out of each side for the ears. Some of them were covered with rings, like the war crown, and most of them had a pair of long tassels sprouting out of the top.

Even a well-trained army will lose battles if it is badly led. In the last battle with the Hittites, the battle of Kadesh in 1286 B.C., Rameses II led the Egyptians into an

ambush and only just escaped with his life. He was forced
to sign a treaty which made the Hittites masters of Syria.
After Kadesh, the two nations never fought again.

The long war had weakened both of them. The Hittite
Empire was destroyed by invaders from the north in the
twelfth century B.C. The Egyptian Empire was lost under
weak rulers, set up by the priests and noblemen. The two
greatest powers in the Ancient World had gone and a
new one was rising in the East.

It was Assyria, the last of our four warrior nations.

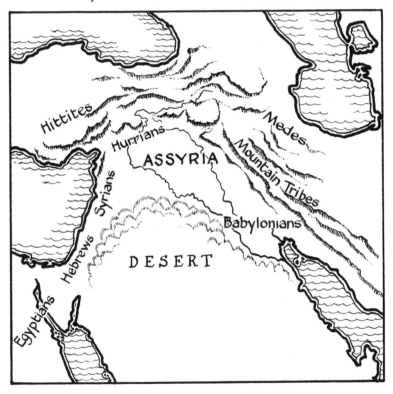

Assyria was like many nations cut off from the sea. She could not grow. The best way for a nation to grow is to send out colonists to find fresh land across the sea. Assyria could not do that. Another way is to invade neighboring countries and take over their land. Assyria could not do that either. She was surrounded by more powerful nations. She could not invade them, she could not break through them to the sea, and, what is worse, she could not stop them from breaking in. Sumerians, Hittites, and Babylonians all ruled in Assyria at one time or another.

Three times the Assyrians thought they saw their chance to break out. The first time was in the twelfth century B.C. The Hittite Empire had fallen and Egypt was weak. But the Syrians were still strong and they threw Assyria back. In the eleventh century, they tried again and failed when the hill tribes invaded them from the north. They had to wait two more centuries for their third and last chance.

Centuries of never-ending war had turned the Assyrians into a fighting machine. Centuries of waiting had made them harsh and cruel. When their last chance came, in the ninth century B.C., they raged across the Middle East, burning, looting, and destroying. By the eighth century, they had conquered Babylonia, Syria, Palestine, and Egypt. They were the greatest empire builders of the Ancient World—and the most hated.

In the beginning, the Assyrian army was a peasant

army led by the king. By the ninth century, it had become one of the greatest fighting machines in the history of the world.

It had every kind of fighting man known to the Ancient World, and one new type, cavalry, as well. Assyrian soldiers used every kind of weapon known to the Ancient World and invented some new ones. And the Assyrians were the first people to have both weapons and armor made of iron.

As we saw, iron was scarce and costly in the beginning. Most of it came from Asia Minor, from the empire of the Hittites. The first great ironsmiths were a tribe called the Chalybes who lived on the northern coast of Asia Minor. (They were so famous that the Greeks called steel *chalybos* after them.) About 1400 B.C., the Chalybes discovered how to turn iron into steel. As their smiths heated the iron in order to shape it, the outside picked up carbon from the charcoal of the furnace. This mixed with the iron and turned it into steel. This is called case hardening, because only the outside or case is steel while the inside is still iron. Case-hardened iron is much stronger than bronze, and it was with this discovery that the Age of Iron really began.

When the Hittite Empire broke up, many of the Chalybic ironsmiths fled to other countries. They taught their skills to other peoples. By 1000 B.C., iron was being used everywhere and it was much cheaper than before. The Assyrians were the first nation to use it for war in a big way. Many ironsmiths had settled in Assyria and many more had been brought back as prisoners of war. Yet, strangely enough, Assyria is poor in iron. Supplies had to be brought from the mountains to the north and east, or from Syria and Asia Minor. Defeated nations were made to pay a yearly fine of iron, as well. But, as the Assyrian army grew, so did the need for more and more iron. This may have been one of the things which led the Assyrians in the ninth century B.C. to break out and begin their bloody conquest of the Middle East.

The iron army of Assyria was made up of chariots; mounted archers and spearmen; foot archers and spearmen; and light troops, slingers, engineers, and armorers. The troops came from Assyria, from her allies, from the nations of her empire, and from captured enemy troops who were forced to fight for the Assyrians.

The king and his noblemen manned the chariots. Each chariot was drawn by a team of two horses and had a crew of three men: a driver, an archer, and a shield bearer. It had square wooden sides and huge eight-spoked wheels, studded with iron round the rim. There were spare quivers attached to the outside, and a holder for a spear and an axe on the inside.

The bow was the layered bow of wood and horn. It seems to have been more powerful than earlier kinds, because the archer pulled the string back to his ear. Besides the bow, the charioteers all carried a straight slashing sword hung on the left hip by a belt over the shoulder.

Assyrian King and Shield Bearer

It was worn higher than the waist and stuck straight out behind, so that the end did not catch on the chariot rail.

The charioteers, the foot archers, the foot spearmen, and the engineers were covered with armor from head to toe. The king had a special helmet shaped like a flower pot turned upside down, with a short spike coming out of the top. The others wore a high, pointed helmet, shaped like a lemon cut across the middle. It was made of iron or copper, with bands of metal running round the bottom to strengthen it. Curved bands shaped like arches ran across the front. Large oval earflaps hung down on each side. They probably had strings attached to them which were tied under the chin to keep the helmet on. The inside of the helmet was lined with leather covered with a thick layer of felt to soften the blows.

A hood was attached to the bottom of the helmet and hung straight down to the shoulders. It had a round facehole in front, which left just the eyes and nose uncovered. The body armor was a long tunic which went down to the ankles. It had short sleeves and was held in at the waist by a wide belt.

The hood and the tunic were covered with rows of small iron plates. These were about two inches long and one inch wide. Some had a rectangular shape, and some had rounded bottoms and ridges down the middle. They were fastened on so that they touched but did not overlap one another. Between the rows of plates, there were rows of knots. These allowed the tunic and hood to bend with the man who was wearing them. If they had not been there, the plates would have jammed against each other and stopped the man from bending at all. They may have been used also to tie on the plates.

In some wall carvings, the rounded plates are shown with the rounded part on top. This was probably the mistake of the carver, because it does not make much sense as armor. Or maybe he knew the right way to show them but thought they looked better upside down.

The tunics must have been laced up the back. They would have been much too stiff to slip over the head, and a sword or spear point could easily slide through an opening in the front, since most of the soldiers did not carry shields. Actually, we do not know what sort of fastening was used because the Assyrians always showed people from the side.

The rest of the army wore the same kind of lemon-shaped helmet without the hood. They had a shorter type of plated tunic which only came down to the hips. It was worn over a woolen tunic which went down to the knees. The legs were protected by padded leggings which were probably tied round the waist under the tunic. They were also tied below the knee to stop them from slipping. Calf-length leather boots were worn over the leggings.

The light troops wore helmets and wool tunics. These helmets were made of iron or copper. They fitted closely to the head. Some were simple skullcaps coming down

Assyrian Cavalry Archer

to the ears. Some were skullcaps with round earflaps. Some had longer sides with a short cheekguard in front of the ear, and a neckguard. They were fitted with crests. These had some kind of flat or curved wooden holder on a short stem and a brush or fan of horsehair.

Over the tunic, they wore wide cross belts which held up the scabbard of the sword. Where the belts crossed on the chest, there was an iron disc, several inches wide, which covered the heart.

The chariot archers and the foot archers had shield carriers to cover them while they shot their arrows. The charioteer's shield was made of wood and sharply curved. The front was covered with heavy metal studs. The foot archer's shield was carried by a spearman. It was a round shield about three feet across, made of wicker or narrow wooden boards covered with leather. It slanted out to a point in the middle. The point was an iron boss, and the rims were bound with iron too.

The cavalry archers had no shields. They dismounted to shoot, while a lancer held the horse.

During a siege, most of the archers fought on foot. They sheltered behind high, thick shields made of bundles of reeds bound together. These shields were about six feet high and stood on the ground. The tops were curved back over the archers' heads to catch arrows and darts dropping from above.

The Assyrians' main weapon was, of course, the layered bow. Their archers had learned to shoot in volleys from the Egyptians. Almost every man had a sword. The Assyrian sword was a professional soldier's weapon. It had a short cut-and-thrust blade of iron. The hilts were only a little wider than the blade and curved up toward it. They were often shaped into lions or bulls or rams' horns.

The spearmen and lancers carried a long spear with a narrow iron head. (The Assyrians were the first people to use the spear as a lance. They were the first people to have real cavalry. During their years as empire builders, the cavalry became more and more important and finally far outnumbered the chariots. Even so, they never got around to inventing either the saddle or the stirrup. Their horsemen rode on a blanket like the American Indians.)

The bow, the sword, and the long spear were the Assyrians' main weapons, but they also used single and double-headed axes, stone and iron maces, daggers (which were often beautifully made and decorated), and slings.

They also had nonfighting troops attached to the army. These were the engineers and the armorers.

The Assyrian army was the first army to have regular engineers. It spent a lot of time besieging cities because no one wanted to fight it in the open. The engineers became a very important part of the army as a result. They were highly skilled at siege craft. They seem to have invented the battering ram and the idea of building an earth ramp up to a city's walls and marching over the top. Their battering ram was an enormous machine. It was moved up to the walls inside a long wooden shed on wheels. At the front of the shed was a tall tower, from which archers could shoot down the defenders on the city walls and prevent them from hurling rocks down on the heads of the engineers below.

The engineers also built roads and bridges, and laid out the army's camp. An Assyrian camp was like a small town. It was surrounded by a high fence of sharp stakes with a tower at each corner. Inside the fence were all the things the army needed to keep it going—even bakeries for making bread.

The armorers were important people, too, in an army that used so much armor, and used it so often. The Assyrian armorers were first-class craftsmen, skilled in working copper, bronze, iron, and precious metals. They had steel tools, and it is surprising how modern the list sounds: hammers, chisels, saws, punches, files, and center bits for boring holes.

They must also have had large factories to turn out as much armor as quickly as they did. They had many new ways of handling iron. (The most important was a quick way to harden it, by quenching it, that is by plunging the red-hot metal into cold water.) They were skilled at shaping armor into curves so that weapons slid off instead of biting into it. These curves are called "glancing surfaces." The craft of making glancing surfaces was one of the armorer's most important skills, all through his history. The Assyrians seem to have been the first to have studied it.

The fame of the Assyrian armorers lasted long after the empire had fallen. The Romans believed that the Assyrians had invented one of the best kinds of armor— mail, which is made of small iron rings looped through each other to make a net. The Assyrians never showed their troops wearing mail; nor did any of the people who came after them, until Roman times. Strange as it seems, it was probably the Romans themselves who invented mail. But the fact that the Assyrians were given the credit shows that the memory of their skill had not faded.

There were other fine craftsmen in Assyria too: architects, sculptors, jewelers, goldsmiths, wall carvers, and mosaic workers. They built and decorated the magnificent palaces that made Nineveh the most beautiful city of its time. The Assyrians also built great roads, had the first postal service, brought cotton into the Western

World, invented the aqueduct, were the first people to write down music, and collected the greatest library of the Ancient World. But they are not remembered for these things.

They are remembered for the cruel and violent way in which they conquered and ruled their empire. They destroyed cities that opposed them. They burned the buildings to the ground, cut down the orchards, and sowed salt into the earth so that crops would never grow again. The people of the cities were tortured and killed, or sent to Assyria as slaves. The men were forced to serve in the Assyrian army.

It was the army that destroyed Assyria as surely as it destroyed her enemies. The country was drained of its wealth to keep the army in action. The peasants were taken from the fields to serve as soldiers and their farms fell idle. Assyria's business was run by foreign traders because her own merchants were busy supplying the army.

In the early part of the seventh century B.C., Medes from the north and Chaldeans from the south invaded Assyria. She was too weak to resist and she was destroyed as violently as any of the nations she had conquered. The capital city of Nineveh was taken and burned.

Two hundred years later, a Greek general called Xenophon marched by the ruins and asked what the name of the city had been and who had built it. And no one could remember.

For sixty years, the Medes took Assyria's place as the most powerful nation in the world. In 549 B.C., a Persian prince, Cyrus, led his peasant archers against them and beat them. Twenty-four years later, his son Cambyses added Egypt to an empire that stretched from India to the Mediterranean. But here the Persians were halted by the infantry armies of a new people in our story, the Greeks. With the Greeks, the second Age of Infantry begins, and our story moves west into Europe.

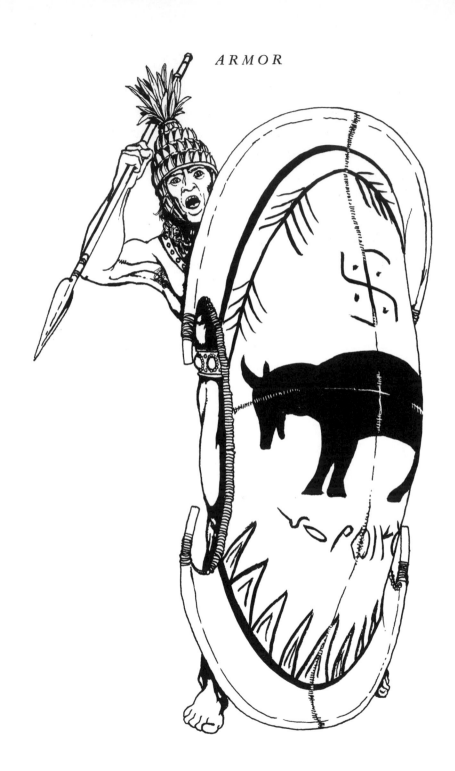

2
The Classical World—Greece

The Greeks loved fighting. Their gods and goddesses were warriors. Their heroes were warriors. Their Bible was a poem about war—the *Iliad* of Homer. They drifted into Greece between 2000 and 1000 B.C. When they had settled in, they began fighting one another.

They came in three great waves from the north. First came the Achaeans (who were true Greeks), who drove out the Myceneans (who were not). The *Iliad* is about one of the battles between them, the siege of Troy. Next came the barbaric Dorians, who drove out the Achaeans and settled in southern Greece. Finally, the Ionians and Aetolians occupied northern Greece. These groups spoke a common language—Greek—and called themselves Hellenes. (They called everyone else barbarians, that is, people who went "baa baa" like sheep instead of talking Greek.)

The Hellenes settled in the valleys and built small cities called *polis*. They were cut off from each other by high mountains. Each polis grew up under its own king with its own special laws and customs. Each one was completely different from the rest. Before long, the Greeks were like strangers to one another. All they had in common was their language and a love of fighting. Wars began between the polis. Greece was never to be free from these wars in all her long history.

The Greeks even formed leagues to fight one another. However, since no Greek could agree with any other Greek for very long, they kept changing sides, until it was difficult to tell who was fighting on whose side and what they were fighting about. Not that the Greeks ever needed a reason to fight. Sparta fought Athens for over a century just to prove that Spartans were better fighters than Athenians.

They were, too. They won the war!

Between wars, the Greeks found time to produce the most brilliant civilization the world has ever seen. Great poets and architects and sculptors appeared everywhere in Greece. Great thinkers arose on all sides, thinkers whose ideas have lived into our own times. Yet, when it came to fighting, the Greeks seemed to run out of ideas. They fought in almost the same way, using almost the same armor, with almost the same weapons for over a thousand years. The Achaean warrior fighting under the walls of Troy in 1192 B.C. would not have looked—or felt—peculiar fighting at the battle of Leuctra in 371 B.C. (Can you imagine Richard the Lion-Hearted charging a Sherman tank? The difference in years between the two is roughly the same.)

The earliest Greek warriors were the Achaeans. The great heroes of the Greeks were the Achaeans who laid siege to Troy in the ten years between 1192 and 1183 B.C. The Greek vase painters of later centuries never tired of painting scenes from the siege of Troy. They appear on hundreds of vases in museums all over the world. But the painters used the warriors of their own times as models. While they show us what a warrior of 500 B.C. looks like, they do not tell us much about the warriors of 1200 B.C. What we do know about them comes mostly from the *Iliad*.

In these earliest days of Greece, most of the fighting was done by kings and noblemen. They rode into battle on chariots and dismounted to fight. The battles consisted of combats between these leaders. What their followers did while they were busy fighting is not very clear. It does not seem to have mattered much—at least, the leaders did not seem to think so.

Their weapons were the spear, the sword, and the bow.

The spear was their favorite weapon. It was to be the favorite of the Greek warriors for the rest of Greece's history. It was six to eight feet long and had a bronze head. It could be used for throwing or for thrusting. If it was thrown, the warrior tried to get it back as quickly as possible. If he could not get it back, or if it was broken, he sent one of his attendants back to camp to fetch another, rather than fight with another kind of weapon. Warfare seems to have been more easygoing then than it is now.

The sword had a double-edged blade of bronze about three feet long, and a bronze handle. It was used mostly as a stabbing weapon. It was carried at the left side on a baldric slung over the right shoulder. The blade was often engraved, or inlaid with precious metals.

The bow was about four feet long. The bowstave was made of wood strengthened at the back with strips of horn and on the front with sinew. It was sometimes covered with a sheath of bark or leather to keep out the damp. The bowstring was made of horsehair and gut twisted together.

The early Greeks did not wear much armor. Instead, they relied on a huge shield, six feet high and four feet wide. It was made of hides stretched on a wooden frame. Sometimes the face was made of bronze for extra strength. It was carried by means of a belt that went around the neck. This left both the warrior's hands free for business.

Shields came in two shapes: rectangular and violin-shaped. The second kind was called a Boeotian shield. It was probably made by stretching the hides over two

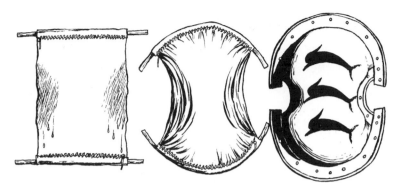

straight pieces of wood after they had been soaked. As the leather dried, it would shrink at the sides and pull the pieces of wood into curves. The frame could then be finished off with crosspieces and rims.

So that there would be no mistake about who was doing all the fighting, the early warriors painted their badges on the front of their shields.

We are told in the *Iliad* that shields were made of four to six layers of hide, and, in at least one case, seven layers. This means that they weighed between 120 and 200 pounds. At one point in the battle, even Ajax, the strongest of the Greeks, had to ask his friends to wait for him because he was too tired to lift his shield.

The tremendous size and weight of the shields led to a strange kind of fighting. When the warrior had dismounted from his chariot, he slung his shield in front of him and began a slanging match with his opponent. The idea was to go on shouting insults until the other man's arm became too tired to hold up his shield, or until he lost his temper and made a false move. Then the spear was driven home. The Greek heroes were as skilled with their tongues as they were with their spear arms.

Helmets were of copper, bronze, or leather. There were two types. The more common was known as the Corinthian helmet, because the people of Corinth always showed the goddess Athene wearing one on their coins. It had a long, wide nasal and wide cheekpieces which practically covered the face. Since it was lined

with leather, it must have been suffocating to wear. When it was not needed, it was pushed up on the back of the head. On top of the helmet was a gay crest of horsehair or feathers. It was dyed a bright color, red and saffron being the favorites. The crest was not worn just for looks; it broke the force of a blow aimed at the top of the head.

The second type of helmet was a strange object called a boar's tooth helmet. Nothing quite like it had appeared before nor has appeared since this period. It was a high, pointed leather cap with rows of wild boar's teeth sewn onto it from top to bottom. The top ended in a knob to which the crest was attached.

Greaves were made from thin sheets of bronze or tin. They fitted closely to the leg and were held in place by the spring of the metal. (If you want to find out for yourself how this worked, take an empty cardboard container like the one used for household cleanser. Cut off the top·and bottom. Slit it down the side from top to bottom and push it onto your leg, or your arm if it is too narrow for your leg.)

With their great shields, these early warriors hardly needed any other armor. The only body armor they had was a wide belt called a mitra. It was made of leather covered with bronze plates or studs to strengthen it. It protected the stomach, which was the most painful place to be wounded, and helped to take the strain of carrying the huge shield.

From 1000 to 650 B.C., the Greek polis were ruled by kings, and for another century and a half by nobles and tyrants. After the kings had gone, the Greeks took to the sea and became merchants as well as farmers. As the common people became richer, the nobles became less powerful. By 500 B.C., the polis had become democracies.

The wealth of the merchant Greeks also brought about a tremendous growth of industry. By the sixth century

B.C., bronze was so cheap that most Greek citizens could afford weapons and armor. Even fighting had become democratic.

Because of this, the style of fighting changed. The foot soldier became all-important, in particular the heavily armed spearmen called hoplites. Chariots and cavalry almost disappeared from the battlefield. Bowmen, slingers, javelinmen, and other light-armed troops became unimportant.

Though the kind of fighting men changed, Greek ideas about fighting did not. Every Greek saw himself as an Achilles, beating whole armies single-handed and covering himself with glory. Bravery in battle was the highest virtue. Only battle heroes went to Olympus, the Greek Heaven, when they died; everyone else went to a dim and dismal place called Hades. In politics, only a successful general could get to the top. You still had to be a fighter to get anywhere in Greece. Things had not changed much since the eleventh century B.C.

Armor did change quite a lot between the eleventh century and the sixth.

The huge shields of the previous age were exchanged for smaller ones, about three and a half feet across. They were either round or Boeotian in shape. Some hoplites liked the Boeotian so much that they had one painted on their round shields. Shields were still made of wood and leather in the same way. Instead of being slung round the neck, they were carried on the left arm by means of

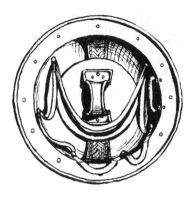

two loops at the back. The arm was slipped through one loop, in the middle, and a second loop at the edge was grasped in the hand. When the hoplite charged, he had to hold his shield at shoulder height, level with the ground. Otherwise it would have banged against his knees and tripped him.

Personal badges were no longer used. Instead, the hoplite painted his city badge on his shield: an owl for Athens, a club for Thebes, and so on.

With the smaller shield, the hoplite needed body armor. The cuirass—*thorax* in Greek—came into use. At first, it was shaped like a barrel and came down to the bottom of the ribs. It was made up of a breastplate and backplate of bronze or leather. The leather was boiled in wax or oil until it was soft, from which it is called cuirbouilli, which simply means boiled leather. While the leather was still wet, it could be molded like papier mâché and made to fit exactly to the hoplite's body.

41

When it dried, it became as hard and as tough as iron. It was a popular kind of armor with foot soldiers in all ages because it was as strong as most metal armor but much lighter.

The two plates of the thorax were fastened together at the shoulders and the waist with straps or thongs. To keep them even more firmly in place, a studded leather belt called a *zoster* was worn round the waist. A kilt of felt or leather flaps, called *pteryges* or "feathers," hung from the zoster and covered the stomach and thighs. Under the kilt was the mitra.

Sometimes, leather thoraxes were made in one piece. They fastened down the front or on the left side under the shield arm with leather laces.

The greaves had not changed except that, since the hoplite had to do a lot more running than the early warriors, they were fastened firmly to the leg by thongs or straps at the back.

The boar's tooth helmet had disappeared but the Corinthian helmet was still popular. Two new kinds of helmet had also come into use: the Athenian and the Spartan. The Athenian helmet, so-called because the goddess Athene always wore one on the coins of Athens, was like the Corinthian but more open. It had a smaller nasal and the cheekpieces were on hinges so that they could be swung up clear of the face. The Spartan helmet was a simple cap with no crest. This suited the Spartans, who had no time for fripperies.

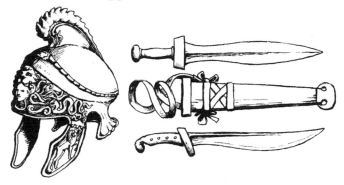

The hoplite used only two weapons, the spear and the sword. The only change in the spear was that the head was made of iron. The sword blade was made of iron, too, but it was much shorter. By the sixth century, it was about the size of a large kitchen knife—and about as much use in a fight. No wonder the hoplite stuck to his spear.

Cavalrymen wore the same armor as the hoplites, but carried a smaller shield. They had a different sword, called a *machaira*. It was a short cutting weapon with a single edge and a curved blade like a modern machete.

Greek cavalry was never very good. They did not have saddles or stirrups to give them a steady seat for a spear thrust. With a spear only eight feet long, they found it difficult to do any real damage to a phalanx. Also, Greece is too full of mountains for cavalry. However, the real reason why the Greeks never bothered with cavalry, and bowmen too, for that matter, was that they despised any type of fighting which did not let you stand toe-to-toe with the enemy and hack away like the old-time heroes.

The Spartans came nearest to the older style of fighting. They were the first of the Greeks to fight in a phalanx, but long after everyone else had changed they still went into battle without armor, carrying the huge six-foot shields. They seemed to like doing everything differently. When they used armor, it was much heavier than anybody else's. They did not use the normal hoplite's sword but had their own special machaira, smaller than the cavalry version. Spartans always had to do things the hard way.

The Spartans lived a hard life. Their country was poor farmland. To get enough to eat, they had to conquer their next-door neighbors, the Messenians. Then they found that, to keep the Messenians from rebelling, every Spartan had to become a soldier. There were so few Spartans—only eight thousand in the fifth century B.C.—that even girls had to train as well as boys.

Weak Spartans were not allowed to live. Sickly or weak babies were killed. Spartan boys were taken from their homes when they were seven and lived together, training to be warriors. The girls were trained to fight, too, until it was time for them to marry and raise a new crop of Spartan soldiers. The boys lived like this until they were twenty-one. Then, if they were good enough, they became Spartan soldiers. (Those who were not led miserable lives.) They had nothing of their own. They were not allowed to eat at home, even if they were married, to trade, or to own gold or silver. Their money was made of iron bars because iron is worthless compared with gold, which was used by the other Greeks. No Spartan would bother to hoard his money and keep it from his fellow Spartans since even a small fortune meant he would have to find a hiding place for tons of iron bars. Spartans were not allowed to run away from a battle. No one would have anything to do with a coward, even his wife and children. No one spoke to him except to curse him and call him names. No wonder the Spartans preferred to die rather than to run away.

Spartan women were as tough as the men. Mothers taught their sons to die well for Sparta. When they went to battle, their mothers would tell them to come back "with their shields or on them." That means that they had to win or to die trying; soldiers who ran from a battle threw away their shields so that they could run faster. Only the victors brought their shields home. Dead sol-

Fifth-Century Hoplite

diers were carried from the battlefield on their shields by their comrades.

The Spartans hated and feared and despised the other Greeks, especially the beauty-loving Athenians. There was no room for beautiful things in the grim and narrow life of Sparta. Though her armies were the best in Greece, Sparta left nothing behind her except the story of a people who made themselves live ugly, hard, and pointless lives, and the word we use to describe anything harsh or bare or uncomfortable—the word "Spartan."

From the sixth century B.C. on, armor changed little. Some improvements were made, however.

The thorax was made longer; it came down to the waist. This meant that the mitra was no longer needed. The kilt of pteryges was attached to the bottom of the thorax itself, instead of to the zoster. There were several layers of flaps. They were longer and covered more of the thighs. Thoraxes of scale armor became common. The scales were either rounded like fish scales or square. They were sewn in overlapping rows onto a tunic of leather or some kind of heavy cloth. Sometimes the whole tunic was covered with scales, sometimes only the bottom half. Shoulderpieces were added to the thorax. They were hinged to the backplate of metal thoraxes. In the case of leather thoraxes, they were made in one piece with the backplate. They were held in place across the shoulders by thongs which were tied to a ring on the front of the thorax.

Shields, helmets, greaves, and weapons remained pretty much the same for the next four hundred years.

In the sixth century B.C., the craft of working in bronze reached its peak in Greece. Like everything else in Greece, the hoplite's armor was beautifully made. Thoraxes and greaves were cunningly shaped to the wearer's muscles. Helmets were made in a variety of shapes and decorated with engraved or embossed designs.

Beautiful or not, the hoplite's armor weighed nearly eighty pounds. Until the fighting started, it was carried by a slave. The hoplite did not wear it any more than he had to.

The only military training the hoplite had was the athletic sports that the Greeks loved. He spent much of his spare time running, leaping, wrestling, boxing, and throwing the discus and the javelin. He kept up his energy on a very slim diet—olives, fresh vegetables, fish (sometimes), and, most of all, barley or wheat made into a kind of porridge. A famous scholar said that dinner in Ancient Greece had two courses: the first was a kind of porridge and the second was a kind of porridge. To drink, there was very strong, heavy wine which was always mixed with water. The Greeks always looked down upon the Romans as a race of drunkards because they drank their lighter wines unmixed.

For all their strength and courage, the Greek warriors failed as fighting men. They were great fighters, but they put personal glory before the dull business of winning battles. When they clashed with the highly trained and disciplined Roman legions, they were defeated. Their kind of fighting had become out of date and it was too late for them to change. Not that they would have wanted to change, even if they had been given the chance.

The Greeks passed into history leaving the world completely altered—except that they added nothing to the science of war.

The Legionary

3
The Classical World— Rome

While Greece was being invaded by the Dorians and their relations, Italy was being invaded in the same way. By the eighth century B.C., the new owners had sorted themselves out and divided up the land among them. The most powerful of the invading tribes was the Etruscans. One of the least important was the Latins, who were sheepherders and farmers living in the hills to the south of them. In the early part of the eighth century, some of the Latins came down to the plain and built a city on the River Tiber. They called the city Rome.

The Romans were not a warlike people. They fought only when they had to. They were farmers at heart, and like all farmers they hated war. War meant that crops would be burned and cattle stolen. War meant that men would be away fighting when they were needed to bring in the harvest. But, like it or not, the Romans had to go to war. So they learned to fight better than anyone else.

Two things helped them. First, they were never too proud to learn from their mistakes. When they were defeated in battle, they found out where they had gone wrong and changed things to make sure that they did not go wrong again. When they came across better armor or better weapons than their own, they were smart enough to borrow the idea. Second, though the farmer and the soldier are enemies, the soldier has to be like the farmer in many ways. He has to be patient, hardworking, obedient, tidy, and tough. Most of all, he is able to keep trying when everything is going wrong.

Because they were farmers, the Romans were all these things. That is why they made good soldiers.

Rome was in trouble from the beginning. The Etruscans took the city soon after it was founded. They built strong walls around it. (The Romans dated their history from that year, 753 B.C. They forgot that the city had been built before the Etruscans took it.) Etruscan kings ruled there for over two hundred years. In 510 B.C., the Romans threw out the kings and Rome became a republic. The Etruscans tried to take Rome back. Other tribes joined in the fight. The Romans had to spend the next 250 years fighting all the tribes in Italy. Enemies came from outside Italy, too: Gauls from across the Alps, Illyrian pirates from across the Adriatic, and Carthaginians from across the Mediterranean Sea. Somehow, the Romans managed to beat them all. By 266 B.C., they ruled all Italy and Sicily. By the year of Christ's birth, the Roman Empire stretched from Britain to India. The army that did all this had to be better than any other.

The Roman army in the days of the Empire was very different from the army in the days of the Etruscan kings. The story of Roman armor is the story of how that army changed and grew.

Under the kings, the fighting was done by the noblemen. A nobleman was any citizen who had land worth at least 120,000 asses—which were copper coins worth about twelve cents, not donkeys—or 100 cows—real cows, that is. They fought in a phalanx eight ranks deep like the Greek hoplites. There were about 3,000 men in the army, split up into three regiments. This tiny army became too small to defend Rome. The rule was changed so that a citizen who had any land at all was allowed to join the army. In the sixth century B.C., the rule was changed again. An important nobleman called Servius Tullius divided the Romans into five classes. The First Class was the richest and the Fifth Class was the poorest. Each class had to raise a certain number of centuries (hundreds) of men for the army. Strict rules were laid down as to how much armor and what weapons each class was to use. These troops were all infantry. In addition, the noblemen provided mounted hoplites. The common citizens, who did not own land, raised five centuries of trumpeters and engineers.

All these troops were divided into two armies. One was of older men whose job was to defend the city. The other was of young men who did all the marching and fighting in the field. Each army was made up of two legions. The word legion came from an older word meaning to choose. In early days, four men would be sent up, and an officer of the first legion was given a chance to pick out the best of the four. Then four more men, and another officer was given first choice; and so on, in turn, until all the men had been chosen. It was like choosing sides for touch football. However, from Servius' time on, the word *legion* simply meant a division of the army.

The first three classes were armored troops. They fought in a phalanx six ranks deep. The front rank was made up of the heavily armored troops of the First Class. The Fourth and Fifth classes were used as skirmishers. They were called *rorarii*.

The legion was commanded by a consul. He was a member of the Roman Senate and was chosen for the job of general by the other members. He picked out six men to help him run the legion. They were called tribunes and one of their jobs was choosing the men for the legions. However, they were not real soldiers; they wanted to use the fact that they had served in the army to get votes later on and become members of the Senate themselves. A man who had not been a soldier did not get votes in Rome. (This is still true today. Over half of the Presidents of the United States of America have been soldiers. Ten have been generals.) Each century was commanded by a centurion. Centurions were chosen from the men of the legion for their strength and courage. They carried a stick of vinewood called a vitis. They used it to keep their men smart and lively and to beat those who broke the rules.

None of the troops were paid until the end of the fifth century. In 406 B.C., the Romans laid siege to the Etruscan city of Veii. The Senate decided to pay the legions to fight on through the winter, rather than let the Veiians get away.

The Romans first ran into the Gauls at about the same time. The Gauls were fast-moving mounted spearmen. They always attacked in a mad rush, yelling and beating their weapons on their shields. The phalanx was too slow and clumsy to meet these crazy charges. The Romans thought about the problem for some time and came up with an answer to it. They got rid of the phalanx, and spread the legion out in three widely spaced lines. The legionaries had room to dodge the flying hoofs and, if the line was broken, could close up again quickly instead of becoming a mixed-up mob as the phalanx did.

The Roman general who finally beat the Gauls was Marcus Furius Camillus. He improved on the three-line legion. Instead of single lines of men, he used lines of maniples, or handfuls. Maniples were squads of 120 men who stood in a block 12 men long and 10 men deep.

In Camillus' legion, each man's place was fixed not by

how much armor he could afford, but by how long he had been in the army. The front line, who were called *hastati,* were men in their twenties. The second line, or *principes*, were men in the prime of life. The third line, or *triarii,* were battle-hardened veterans. The very youngest men, called *velites* or fast movers, became skirmishers. There were ten maniples in each line and ten maniples of velites in each legion.

The maniples of the first two lines had gaps between them. The principes were placed so that they covered the gaps in the hastati. The triarii and velites stood to-

gether in a solid line. In the next century, the triarii were spread out like the front lines and covered the gaps in the principes. The velites opened the battle and then took cover behind the legion.

The new Roman battleline looked like a checkerboard. The Romans called it a *quincunx.* This was the Latin word for the five-spot on dice: take a look at one and you will see why the Romans used it. The quincunx was a very efficient battleline. It usually attacked in three waves as each line went into action. The enemy had no time to get over one attack before the next one hit him. If a heavier attack was needed, the principes could easily move into the gaps in the hastati to make a phalanx. One wing of the legion could attack while the other held its ground without throwing the whole legion into confusion. This would have been impossible with a phalanx.

The quincunx was just as good in defense. If the hastati got into trouble, they could retreat through the gaps in the principes and leave the enemy facing a line of fresh troops. When the enemy attacked, half his men were wasted because they faced the gaps in the line. If they pushed through the gaps, their line was broken and they were easily thrown back by the maniples of the line behind.

The legion went through more changes at the end of the second century B.C. The man who made the changes was another great general, Gaius Marius.

Before Marius' time, the Romans thought that their men would fight harder if they were fighting for their own property. That is why they allowed only landowners to join the army. However, the number of landowners had been getting smaller year by year. Men who had grown rich on the wars of the third and second centuries had started huge farms. They could afford to sell their crops cheaply. Thousands of small farmers were ruined because they could find no market for their goods. They had to give up their land. Some of them went to work for the big farmers; many more drifted to the cities to try to make a living there.

Marius needed these men. So he threw out the land-owning law and made a new one that allowed any Roman citizen to join the legion, whether he owned land or not. In this way, he was able to use the out-of-work farmers. They were happy to be legionaries because they were well paid and the city of Rome gave them food and clothing and a place to live. Besides, as a Roman soldier a man could serve his City and win glory, too.

Marius' new troops were Rome's first full-time soldiers. They signed on for twenty years. They took an oath of loyalty to their general; before Marius, the troops had sworn to serve Rome. This made a general a very powerful man because he practically owned the army that served under him, although Rome paid them and gave them a gift of land when their service was over.

He also gave each legion a name and a battle standard. The standard was a silver model of the Roman eagle on a long pole. Later the eagle was made of gold. It was a great disgrace to let the enemy capture the eagle. Some legions were disbanded because this happened. The stand-ard-bearer was called the aquilifer, or eagle carrier, and was just below the centurion in rank.

The Romans invaded Gaul and Germany about this time. The German tribes were even tougher and wilder fighters than the Gauls. Maniples were too small to stand up to them. Marius brought in a larger unit called a cohort. This was made up of three maniples, or six centuries. There were eighty men in each century and sixty cen-

Aquilifer

turies in each legion, divided into ten cohorts. The cohorts still fought in the quincunx: four in the first line and three in each of the others.

The cohorts were numbered from right to left and from front to back. The First Cohort was on the right of the front line and the Tenth was on the left of the third line. The centuries in each cohort were numbered in the same way. The top centurion, who was called the primus pilus or first ranker, was in command of the First

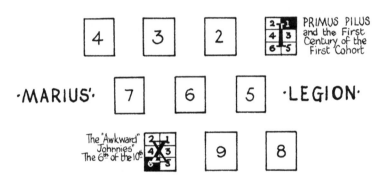

Century of the First Cohort and his men were the best in the legion. The lowest-ranking centurion commanded the Sixth Century of the Tenth Cohort. His men were usually raw recruits and the "awkward Johnnies" of the legion.

Marius was able to use these big cohorts because, with the stiff training they got, six hundred legionaries could move and fight like one man. The centurions saw to the training. In the new legions, they were the most important men. Even with bad generals, the Roman army was hard to beat because of the centurions; with a good general like Marius or Julius Caesar, they were unbeatable.

The velites disappeared. Light infantry, and all other special troops, came from the allies of Rome or were hired barbarians. Cavalry came from Gaul, archers from Egypt and Crete, slingers from the Balearic Islands. These non-Roman troops were called auxilia, or helpers. A legion of auxilia was always attached to a legion of Roman infantry.

During the first century B.C., artillery was added to the legion. This consisted of catapults and huge bows which were used mostly at sieges. The biggest catapults could hurl two-hundred-pound rocks over a quarter of a mile. The bows shot great darts and arrows the same distance.

For the next two hundred years, the main work of the legions was guarding the borders of the Empire. But things were changing for the worse. Fewer of the legionaries were coming from Rome itself, although the legionaries still had to be Roman citizens. They came mostly from the provinces. Training turned them into fine soldiers, but the old spirit was gone. In the third century, the Emperor Caracalla made every freeman living within the borders of the Empire a Roman citizen. When these new "Roman" citizens came into the legions, they brought their own ways of fighting with them. They could not be trained in the true Roman way. The army became an unruly mob. When hordes of barbarians from Asia swept into Europe in the third century, the legions could not keep them out. The emperors had to hire barbarians to fight barbarians. This was the deathblow to what had once been the greatest army in the world. It quickly fell apart. The Roman Empire was overrun and Europe moved into the Dark Ages.

Now that we have seen how the Roman army grew, we can go back and take a look at the armor and the weapons that it used.

The noblemen, who fought under the Etruscan kings, had the same armor and weapons as the Greek hoplites: Corinthian helmets, short bronze thoraxes, bronze or tin greaves, and a short sword and long spear. These had been copied from the Greeks by the Etruscans, who passed them on to the Romans. Only the shield, which was called a *clipeus*, was different. It was the same shape and size as the hoplite's, but it was flatter. It was made of wood covered with bronze, and had a single metal handle.

The Athenian helmet and the long thorax appeared soon after they came into use in Greece. When the five classes started, this type of armor was worn by the troops of the First Class.

The Second and Third classes had to have metal armor, too, but they used native Italian armor. The Second Class had to have a helmet, greaves, and a shield; the Third, only a helmet and shield.

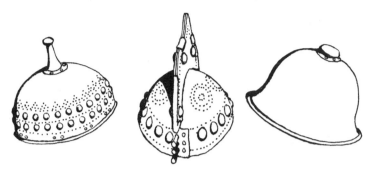

There were several types of Italian helmet. The most common ones were a simple pot-shaped helmet with a spike on top, and a helmet shaped like a bell. Another type is called the bivalve, because it was made of two curved pieces of bronze like an oyster shell. (Oysters belong to the bivalve family of shellfish. The Romans were very fond of them. The best oysters came from a little town called Colchester in Britain. Colchester oysters were shipped all the way to Rome.) The two pieces of the bivalve helmet were welded and riveted into a high pointed headpiece. Where they joined, a tall, flat metal crest was formed. The top of the crest was the same shape as the headpiece. Between the end of the crest and the rim of the helmet, there were three short rods, one above the other. Why they were there is a mystery.

Other helmets were made of metal or leather strips woven over and under like cloth. Some were made of pottery. They were cheap to make, but a soldier wearing one of them must have felt strange going into battle with an upturned flower pot on his head.

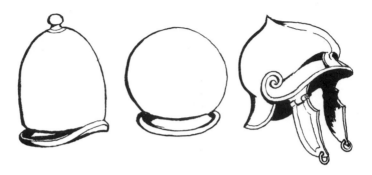

In the fifth century, three new types of helmets replaced them. The first looked like a smooth beehive. The second looked like a round goldfish bowl, upside down. The third was a sort of cousin of the Corinthian helmet. It looked like a small Corinthian helmet perched on top of the head with long, narrow cheekpieces coming down from it. The bottom of the "Corinthian" helmet was really the rim of the headpiece and made a peak just above the eyebrows. It had a tuft of feathers or horsehair for a crest. All of these helmets were tied under the chin with leather strips. The strips were riveted to the helmet just in front of the ears.

Second Class troops also wore bronze chest protectors called pectorals. These came in three different shapes. The most common was an oblong with sides that curved in slightly. It was about twelve inches wide and nine inches high. It was lined with leather. Straps went over the shoulders and round the back to hold it in place. The second type was a disc about five inches across. Three of these were riveted to a piece of leather and held on with

Second Class
Legionary

straps. The third type was shaped like a baby's bib, with a curved top which fitted tight round the neck.

Pectorals were covered with decoration. Sometimes they were made of gold, or covered with a thin layer of gold. The decorations were magic signs, made of patterns of rivets, which were supposed to turn aside enemy weapons. There were circles (the sign of the sun), crescents (for the moon), thunderbolts, and many more. Sun symbols were supposed to keep away poisoned arrows. It is hard to tell how well they worked, because no one was using poisoned arrows at the time.

Fourth Class troops had to have only their shield and weapons; Fifth Class troops only their weapons. Neither class wore metal armor. The Fifth Class went into battle in their everyday tunics, their heads bare. Fourth Class troops had tunics of leather or padded cloth, and caps of leather or felt. Some of them wore the heads of wild beasts—wolves or bears—as helmets. They were fine for scaring the enemy, but they must have given off a terrible smell.

The Second, Third, and Fourth classes used a shield called a *scutum*. This was oval or rectangular in shape, and slightly curved for better cover. It was about five feet long and two feet wide. At first, it was made of wicker or of small boards nailed to a wooden frame. In the sixth century, it was made of two pieces of wood, glued back to back. The grains of the wood ran crosswise to each other, like plywood. This stopped the shield from splitting if it was hit on the edge. The front was covered with leather, often calfskin, and strengthened with a wide strip of bronze, running from top to bottom. There was an oval wooden boss in the middle, with a metal strip across the back for a handle.

The first three classes used the Greek sword and a long spear called a *hasta*. The Fourth Class had the Greek sword and a javelin, called a *verutum*, which means a cooking spit. This was about four feet long. It had a wooden shaft and a bronze head, five inches long. The Fifth Class had the verutum, or darts, or a slingshot.

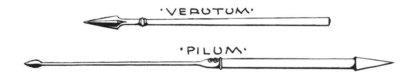

·VERUTUM·

·PILUM·

In the fifth century, a better javelin appeared. It was called a *pilum*. It became one of the legion's most important weapons. It had an iron head four feet long, and a handle of cornel wood the same length. (Cornel wood is a tough kind of dogwood.) The head was a thin shaft with a leaf-shaped blade at one end, and a flat tongue at the other. The flat end was pushed into a slot in the handle, and riveted with two bronze pins. Later a socket was used to join the head to the handle. It fitted over the end of the handle and was riveted in the same way. Where the handle joined the head, it was thickened for about nine

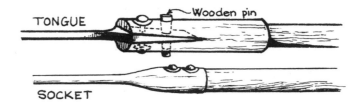

inches to give a firm throwing grip. The bottom of the handle was sharpened and tipped with iron. This was done so that the legionaries could turn their pila round and use them as pikes against cavalry. (The thin iron shaft of the pilum would have bent under the weight of a horse.)

One strange thing about the pilum is that the Romans never showed what it looked like in all their carvings of battles and armies. What we know about it comes from Roman writers, and from a few rusty pilum heads dug up on ancient battlefields.

The beginning of the fourth century was a time of great change for the Roman army. Camillus had more to do with this than anyone else. He began the task of giving the Romans a professional army.

First, he made all the legionaries wear metal helmets. For the first time, the Romans had to face slashing weapons, which were aimed at the top of the head. These were the unpointed double-edged swords of the Gauls. Leather and cloth were no protection against them. The Romans began a long search for the perfect helmet: one that was strong, light, and easy to make.

Next, Camillus made all the legionaries use the oval scutum. This had been improved. The edges of the shield were bound with iron. It was carried by two loops, one for the arm and the other for the hand. A long strap had been added so that the scutum could be slung on the back, out of the way, when it was not needed.

Next, he armed the first two ranks with the pilum. Only the triarii kept the hasta. Later, because the pilum was such a good weapon, the whole legion used it.

The Romans discovered two new types of armor, which soon replaced all others: scale armor, which they got from the Greeks; and ring armor, which they got from the Gauls.

Roman scale armor was copied from the hoplite's. Bronze scales were sewn to a leather tunic with wire or leather thread. They were oval or diamond-shaped and about two inches long. The wire or thread passed through a small hole in the top of the scale. Each scale overlapped the next, and each row half covered the one below.

Ring armor was invented by the Gauls. Bronze or iron rings, about an inch across, were sewn in rows onto a tunic, with fine wire or thread. Sometimes both types of armor were used together. The chest and shoulders were covered with scales and the rest with rings.

These tunics were fastened at the shoulder. The fastening was covered by leather shoulderpieces which were riveted to the back of the tunic and tied with thongs in front.

Pectorals were still being used. At first, they were worn over the armor tunic. Later, because the straps slipped on the scales and rings, they were worn underneath.

Both types of armor were perfect for the legionary. They were so light that they did not tire him out on his long marches. They were strong but not stiff, like solid armor, so they did not hamper his throwing arm. And any legionary could afford a scale or ring tunic because they were easy and cheap to make.

The armor tunic was called a *lorica*. The word came from a much older one, *lora*, which meant sandal leather. Probably, in the early days, armor was made from the tough leather which the sandalmakers used. The word *lorica* was used for any kind of armor tunic, whether it was made of leather or metal, just like our word "cuirass."

During the fourth century, the Romans tried out two new kinds of helmet. The first was called a Phrygian helmet. It was a lighter kind of Athenian helmet with long, narrow cheekpieces. Instead of a crest, its headpiece

sloped up to make a sharp comb. The comb curled over into a knob at the front like the top of a breaking wave. The men of Phrygia wore a sort of stocking cap which flopped over in the same way. This is where the name came from.

The other new helmet looked like an old-fashioned policeman's helmet. It had a high rounded headpiece with pointed peaks at the front and back. The peaks pointed down a little to cover the face and neck. The crest was a sprout of horsehair or feathers, carried in a holder shaped like the nozzle of a garden hose.

The last idea the Romans borrowed came from Spain. When Hannibal the Carthaginian invaded Italy in 218 B.C., he brought some Celts from Spain with him. Their weapon was an iron sword. The blade was over two feet long and two inches wide. It was shaped by hammering, which made it much stronger than if cast in a mold. It was both pointed and double-edged. The hilt was a little wider. The handle was built up of layers of leather and metal rings, and ended in a large round knob. The scabbard was made of wood covered with leather. It hung at the right side on a belt which went round the waist.

The Romans saw that it was a much better sword than the Greek sword they had been using. They began to use it themselves, and before long it became the legionary's second weapon. Like the Celts, they wore it on the right side. They used the sword belt to hold in the lorica at the waist, which made it more comfortable to wear. This sword is known as the Hispanic sword, from the Latin word for Spain, Hispania.

Under Camillus, the ordinary men of the legion all wore the same sort of equipment. It was almost like a uniform. The officers began to stand out because their armor was quite different. They wore the "muscled" solid cuirasses, shaped to their bodies, and Athenian helmets with red or black crests. Cuirasses and helmets were often plated with gold and silver and decorated with engravings. The sleeves and skirt of the tunic underneath the cuirass were cut into wide strips which ended in fringes. They were decorated with silver studs.

Centurions' armor was the same as that of the higher officers but was plainer. As a badge of rank, they wore their crests from left to right.

Caesar took his legions into Gaul and Germany. They had to fight more battles and march farther and faster than they had ever done before. Armor had to be stronger and lighter than ever before.

Crests almost disappeared. They added weight to the helmet but did nothing useful.

The Phrygian and the "policeman's" helmets were re-

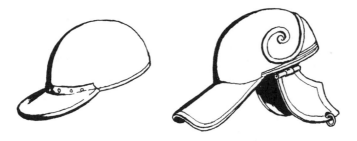

placed by a much lighter, simpler helmet. It was a plain pot with a flat, rounded neckguard sticking straight out at the back. The legionary looked like a baseball catcher when he was wearing it. The only trouble was that, without cheekpieces or a visor, it gave no protection to the face. Also, if the legionary bent his head down at the wrong moment, his neck was left wide open. So the Romans gave up lightness for better protection. A better but heavier helmet took its place. In this, the neckguard came down lower on the neck and was curved down for a "glancing surface." Wide, hinged cheekpieces covered the face and ears. This helmet was better but it still did not cover the neck properly.

The Romans next tried a new type of Athenian helmet. The headpiece was a simple pot shape. The back of the headpiece went straight down to the shoulders. It curved out sharply at the bottom to make a rim about one inch wide. This neckguard covered the neck no matter what the wearer did. Where the neckguard met the headpiece, a round piece was cut out to make room for the ear and

a thick rim ran round the earhole and down the front of the neckguard. The cheekpieces were hinged in front of the earhole. They were the same size and shape as the jaw with an extra bulge in front to cover the cheek-bone.

A crest could be worn for parades and such. Of course, it was always removed for fighting. It was attached by a pin or screw which went through a hole in the top of the headpiece.

The only thing wrong with the helmet was that it did not cover the front of the face. This was soon put right. A peak was added. It was a flat strip about an inch wide which ran around the front of the helmet a couple of inches above the rim. It could move up and down on rivets which held it onto the headpiece. Because it could move like this, it took the force out of a blow to the head, by bouncing when it was hit. This must have saved many a legionary from a headache after a battle. The neckguard was made a little shorter to give more freedom to the neck. It was also curved more sharply and the rim was made wider. The cheekpieces were made wider too but stayed the same length and shape. The crest was fastened differently. It slid into a flat holder and was locked in place with a spring clip. A ring was attached to the neck-guard. On the march, the legionaries carried the helmets slung at the shoulder by a thong which passed through the ring.

Ring and scale loricas were still the favorite armor of the legions. Then, in the first century B.C., mail appeared. It was very crude at first. Each row was made of a single

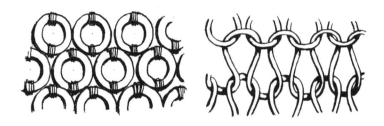

piece of wire, bent up and down into loops like an accordion. Mail soon began to take the place of ring armor, because it had everything that ring armor had, and it was stronger, too. Scale and mail loricas were made in the same way as scale and ring ones had been. Cavalry wore mail loricas split at the sides so that they could straddle their horses.

A very large rectangular scutum took the place of the oval type. It went from the chin to the ankles and curved halfway round the body. It was held by two handles as before. The legionary's name and legion number were cut into the boss and again, on the inside, at the top. He also had the badge of his cohort and of his legion on the front. There was not much chance of a legionary forgetting who he was and where he belonged while he had his shield.

Special troops had their own badges. The Praetorian Guard had a scorpion. Marines had a trident, which stood for Neptune, the sea god. Legions who had done something special were given a badge to wear on their shields in its memory. For instance, troops who had fought against the Gauls or the Germans carried a torque, which was the collar worn by Gaulish and German chieftains. The rest of the space on the shield was filled with magic symbols. Thunderbolts appeared on nearly every shield, and arrows, eagles, and bulls were often used. These badges and signs were cut out of sheets of metal, or cast in molds, and then riveted to the shields.

The legionaries gave up wearing greaves when they began to use the new scutum. It completely covered the legs and made greaves unnecessary.

Marius was a busy man but he still found time to make an improvement in the pilum. His idea was to stop the enemy picking it up and throwing it back at the legionaries. It was a very simple idea. A wooden pin was used in place of one of the metal ones. When the pilum struck, the wooden pin snapped and the handle swung loose on the metal pin.

Julius Caesar had an even better idea. He had the shaft made slightly softer just behind the head. This pilum not only snapped, it bent too. This meant that it could not be pulled out if it stuck in a shield. The enemy soldier had to make a choice between throwing his shield away and dragging it round with ten pounds of bent and broken pilum pulling down his arm and getting tangled up with his feet. Either way, the legionary was happy about it.

Each legionary had two pila. One was heavier than the other. The light one, which could be thrown farther, was let fly at about thirty paces from the enemy. The heavy one, which could do more damage, was thrown at about ten paces. Then the legionary drew his sword and finished the work off with that.

Caesar's adopted son became the first Emperor of Rome in 28 B.C. He took the name Augustus. Augustus brought peace to the Roman world and the legions kept that peace for the next two hundred years. During those years, their main job was to keep the borders of the empire safe from outsiders.

What sort of a man was the legionary?

As we know, he was a Roman citizen and very proud of it. To look at, he was short and stocky, with a dark skin and black hair cropped short. The Romans never cared about how big their soldiers were. They believed that obedience and a sense of order were more important than size. They thought that good health was important, though, and made sure that their soldiers had plenty of exercise and good food.

In peacetime or on garrison duty, the legionary lived in a barracks. He shared a room with seven other men. On the march, he shared a leather tent, ten feet square, with the same men. From this, the unit of eight men got its name of contubernium, or tent party.

Centurions and higher officers had a tent to themselves. Generals often had tents made of silk or some other rich material. Every tent was carried by a packhorse, which meant that nearly seven hundred horses were needed just to carry tents for one legion.

When a citizen reached his seventeenth birthday, he could join the legion and could serve until he was sixty years old. He signed on for twenty years at a time. For the first sixteen years he was an ordinary legionary; for the last four, he was called a veteran. Veterans had a much easier time than the ordinary legionaries. They had their own cohort, their own battle flag, and their own place in camp. More important—to them, at least—they did not have to do any of the chores which took up so much of the ordinary legionary's time. All the veterans had to do was to fight when the time came.

One other kind of legionary was given very special treatment: the evocati, or recalls. The evocati were men who had served their time in the army and retired; they were called back in time of war. That is, if the general could persuade them. Many of them became centurions

Centurion

straight away, because they knew everything about fighting and about soldiering. Their coolness and skill helped to steady new troops who had never been in a battle before.

The ordinary legionaries were kept busy from morning to night. Training took up most of their time: arms drill, target practice, maneuvers, physical exercise, swimming, and so on. In between, they had to clean their equipment, repair and wash their clothes, tidy up the camp or barracks, work in the kitchen or the mess, do guard duty or any one of the many other jobs that had to be done. In enemy territory, they also had to look for food, find packhorses, guard prisoners, do picket duty, make roads, and build forts. And, of course, fight battles.

Everything was done to the sound of a bugle or trumpet. A bugle call woke the legionary (at five o'clock in the morning), told him to start work, called him to his meals, told him the time, and sent him to bed at night.

Three times a month, the legion went on a march of twenty miles, to keep the men in training for war. They marched with all their armor, weapons, and equipment. The ordinary speed of the legion was 100 paces a minute. When they wanted to get somewhere fast, they traveled at 120 paces a minute. They practiced both paces on their training marches, carrying a pack that weighed between thirty and forty-five pounds. The pack contained a spade, a saw, an axe, a basket, a piece of chain, a length of cord, a sickle, and a cooking pot; a bundle of spare clothes and a repair kit; two long wooden stakes to make the fence around their camp; and between one and seventeen days' rations. (One day's rations weighed nearly two pounds.) All this was carried on a long pole with a crosspiece. The legionaries called it "Marius' Mule" because Marius had invented it to help them carry all the gear that he had loaded onto them in the first place. He expected them to be engineers, carpenters, builders, farmers, woodsmen, and cooks as well as soldiers. He made sure they had their tools with them at all times.

The legionary ate very simple food: wheat flour made into bread or porridge, vegetables made into soup, and cheese. He cooked his meals in olive oil or lard. His drink was sour wine, which may not taste very good but is the best thing in the world for quenching a thirst. He did not like meat much; when he did eat it, pork was his favorite.

In peacetime, the general kept his men out of mischief by putting them to work building things. The legionaries built bridges and aqueducts which brought water to the towns and cities. They built canals and public buildings. They built villages for veterans to live in when their fighting days were over. They built roads for the army to march on, and forts for it to live in.

The legionary's life was no easier in wartime.

Every morning, as soon as the baggage was stowed away, the legion marched out of camp. They destroyed it behind them, so that the enemy could not use it. They were supposed to march thirty-five miles by noon—unless they had to fight a battle on the way. Wherever they halted, they built a camp. It was always built to the same plan, so that, if the enemy attacked, every man could find his way to his post without any fuss. The camp was surrounded by a dirt wall with a fence on top. This was made of the stakes the legionaries carried in their packs. There was a tower at each corner of the wall with a catapult on top. Such a camp was built at the end of every day's march while the legions were in enemy country.

Discipline was hard in the legion. Punishment was harsh. Refusing to obey an order, cowardice, or mutiny could be punished by death. If a whole unit had to be punished, every tenth man was put to death. A sentry who slept at his post was stoned by his comrades. Stealing, lying, and laziness were punished by flogging. The centurion gave the beating with his vitis. For less serious crimes, the legionary's rations could be cut or his pay stopped for a time. In wartime, he could be made to sleep outside the camp, where there were no sentries and stout walls between him and the enemy. One punishment was not only painful; it gave the other legionaries a good laugh. The offender was made to march round the camp with his full pack, wearing nothing but his undershirt.

There were rewards as well as punishments. The legionaries were awarded armbands or collars for courage, just as we give medals nowadays. Officers were given crowns. Centurions wore their crowns on a leather harness over their cuirasses. The highest award was the *corona civica,* or citizen's crown, which was given to any soldier who saved a comrade's life in battle.

Victorious generals were rewarded magnificently. They were given a parade through the streets of Rome which was called a triumph. The general was carried in a chariot like the Etruscan kings. He wore a purple robe and a laurel wreath. Behind him came the defeated enemy generals, led by ropes tied round their necks, and carts full of booty. Then came the general's legions in parade armor, eagles gleaming and horns sounding.

The legionary was well paid. Part of his pay was held back for such things as his rations and bedding, repairs to his weapons and armor, and the yearly camp dinner. He bought some of his clothing and his boots from the army, too. With all the marching he did, it is not surprising that he spent so much money on boots. Sometimes, when the marching had been harder than usual, he was given a special allowance to get his boots repaired. After all these things had been paid for, he still had about two-thirds of his pay left. Some of it was put in the savings bank, which was kept by the cohort standard-bearer. The rest went to buy extra food or to bribe the centurion not to give him the worst chores. He liked gambling, too. Dice and jacks were the favorite games. The soldiers at Christ's Crucifixion played dice for His robe.

The legionary had other ways of making money. He shared in the booty when an enemy camp or town was taken. Sometimes when a new Emperor took over and sometimes on an Emperor's birthday he gave gifts of money to the troops. Soldiers often traded in the markets of local towns where they were stationed. Finally, when the legionary left the army at the end of his twenty years, he was given a large bonus as a reward for faithful service to Rome.

Many legionaries had special skills that were needed by the army. These men usually went into the First Cohort. Because of this, it was twice as large as the other cohorts. In it there were armorers and smiths, carpenters and catapult makers, surveyors and architects, boat builders and arrowsmiths, and glassmakers and woodsmen. There were clerks to keep the records and clerks to look after the payroll. There were doctors, usually Greeks, with their assistants and bandage carriers. They were skilled in surgery, and they knew about germ-killers. They used tar and turpentine. On the other hand, they knew next to nothing about medicine. They mixed up horrible herb brews, threw in a few spells, and trusted to luck. So the legionaries kept fit by exercise, cleanliness, and good, plain food and steered clear of the doctors as much as possible.

Each legion also had a corps of engineers who took care of the catapults. Most of these were huge things, used to batter down the walls of towns. Some were smaller, such as those on the camp towers. The smallest were called *carroballista*. These were mounted on pony carts and had a crew of five men. They fired large arrows or nine-inch darts. Each century had its own carroballista. The engineers also built battering rams, siege towers, and bridges of boats. Another of their jobs was to collect all the pilum heads after a battle, so that they could be repaired and used again.

The legionary's clothes were plain and simple. He wore a sleeveless linen undershirt. Over this went a woolen tunic. Last of all came his lorica, held in at the waist by his sword belt. Sometimes he wore a plain linen or leather tunic over his lorica. On his head went an iron skullcap with the helmet over all. When he was not wearing his helmet, he went bareheaded. Round his neck was a woolen scarf. His all-important boots had heavy leather soles, studded with great nails. They were fastened with thongs which went round his ankles and calves. In wintertime, or in cold countries, he wore woolen breeches which came down to the knee. He also wound cloth leggings round his calves and stuffed rags into his boots. (Both these ideas came from the Gauls. Those Gauls again!) Over everything, he wore a reddish-brown wool cloak with a hood, which could cover him from the top of his crest to his ankles.

During the first and second centuries after Christ, the Romans had time to try out many new and different things. They began to decorate armor as they had rarely done before. But no matter what they did to it, Roman armor was always soldiers' armor: for use, not just for show.

The search for the perfect helmet still went on. Many different types of helmets were tried. One of them was the helmet that most people think of as a Roman helmet. It is called the Hagenau helmet after the place in Germany where it was found again after being buried for centuries. The pot-shaped iron headpiece was strengthened with two strips, one going across and the other from front to back. The cheekpieces were long and narrow and very pointed. The neckguard was shaped like a fan and curled down at the sides. It was slanted to give plenty of cover to the neck. Around the bottom of the headpiece was a wide rim. It was wider in front than at the sides, and made a visor about two inches wide over the face. On top of the helmet, where the strengthening strips crossed, there was a kind of crest. It was a ring about two inches across, standing on its edge. This was the magic sign for the sun.

The helmet with the bouncing peak had been changed in several ways. The crest had gone completely. Instead, the headpiece came to a pointed comb on top, running from front to back. The peak was not hinged, it was welded to the helmet, and it stood straight up instead of jutting out over the nose. The cheekpieces were hinged as before, but they were much larger. They covered the ears and curved round to cover most of the face as well. Strangely enough, the earhole was still cut out of the side of the headpiece, even though the ears were covered. The neckguard was shorter and did not curve out so much.

One old favorite came back into use—the Phrygian helmet. Each one seems slightly different from all the rest. Some of them had long wide neckguards, some had short narrow ones; some had wide cheekpieces, some narrow; and so on.

Even the ordinary legionaries' helmets were decorated with engraved designs. Officers' helmets were even richer than before. They were made of solid gold or silver, with designs cut into the metal. Sometimes the designs were made of thin strips of gold or silver or copper hammered into the helmets.

Officers still wore the solid Greek cuirass and greaves, which were usually made of leather in the first century. The cuirasses were decorated with strips of metal cut into fanciful shapes and riveted to the metal. Their shoulderpieces came in all sorts of shapes and were decorated

Consul

with gold and silver studs, shaped like lion heads, stars, or flowers. The thongs holding the shoulderpieces were often painted gold or were made of gold thread and ended in tassels. A row of large rounded scales hung from the bottom of the cuirass and round each armhole. Underneath the cuirass went the tunic with the sleeves and skirt of decorated strips. Cuirass, scales, and strips were often painted red or black to add to the fun.

The legionaries' loricas went through some changes during the first century. They were made in one piece and came down to the waist instead of to the thighs. Shoulderpieces disappeared because they were no longer needed to cover the shoulder fastening. The sleeves and the bottom of the lorica were scalloped; that is, they were cut into half circles or zigzags or squares. The tunic that went over the lorica was a little shorter and was scalloped in the same way. Scale armor was still one of the favorite types of armor. The mixed lorica, in which scale and ring or scale and mail were used together, became less common and finally disappeared.

Mail replaced ring armor more and more. Ring armor loricas had almost disappeared by the end of the first century. One of the main reasons was that real mail, separate links of iron threaded through each other, was being made by the beginning of the second century. Officers sometimes wore a mail tunic underneath their leather cuirass.

A strange new kind of armor appeared at the end of the first century. No one knows exactly when it was first used, where it came from, or how it was put together. It was called the *lorica segmentata,* or sliced-up lorica, because it looked like a solid cuirass cut into neat slices and put back together again. It appears for the first time in a column put up by the Emperor Trajan A.D. 113. The column is covered with scenes of his victory over the Dacians. It looks like a stone cartoon strip. Most of the legionaries on the column wear the lorica segmentata. Other later carvings show that it was used all through the second century. But of all the loricae segmentatae that were made, only a few bent and rusty plates are left today. What little we know about the lorica segmentata comes from this handful of plates and the scenes on the column. Everything else is pure guesswork.

It must have been fairly new in Trajan's time, because the column shows all sorts of fastenings being used. This meant that the Romans were still looking for the best one. However, most of the loricas are made in the same way, so the Romans had had time to settle that, at least.

The lorica was in three parts: two pairs of plates over the top of the chest and back, four or five narrow strips covering each shoulder, and five or six wide strips round the body.

Each pair of plates was hinged in the middle. They were fastened to each other by straps over the shoulders and under the arms. Sometimes, instead of hinges, a thong was used to tie each pair of plates in the middle, or straps and buckles were used. (The Romans invented the buckle

*Legionary
in Lorica Segmentata*

with the tang, or point, which goes through a hole in the strap, in the first century after Christ.)

The shoulder strips were about an inch wide and curved down over the chest and back. They were not fixed to each other, but could move freely when the arm and shoulder were moved. Since they were not fastened at the ends to the rest of the armor, they must have been fastened to the top of the shoulder. However, the fastening is hidden by the strips so we have no idea how this

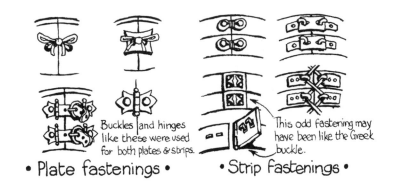

Buckles and hinges like these were used for both plates & strips.

This odd fastening may have been like the Greek buckle.

• Plate fastenings •   • Strip fastenings •

was done. And we never will, unless somebody finds a shoulder strip one day.

The body strips covered the lower part of the chest and the stomach down to the waist. They were flat hoops about two inches wide, made of two pieces hinged together at the back and fastened in front. Many different fastenings were used. Some strips were fastened with a strap and buckle; some with a loop of thong which fitted over a stud on each end of the strip. Sometimes a piece of leather with a small slit in each end was used instead of a thong. One piece of body strip has been found. A hook is welded to it. This type was probably fastened with a long thong which went round each hook, crisscross like the lace of a skating boot, and tied at the bottom. The leather patch may have been used to protect the thong, which could easily be cut by an unlucky blow. In some cases, the strips were hinged in front and fastened in back. A later type of lorica segmentata had strips running right up to the neck instead of chest and back plates.

Another question about the lorica segmentata is how the strips were held in place. They may have been riveted or fastened in some way to a leather tunic; or they may have been attached to a leather harness hanging from the shoulders like suspenders. The centurions sometimes wore a harness to carry their crowns and other awards. Perhaps the strips were fastened to something like that. Again, nobody knows.

A new oval scutum appeared in the first century. It was flatter and smaller than the old scutum. At first, it was used only by the Praetorian Guard and the cavalry. Then, during the second century, the legionaries began to use it as well. They kept the "gladiator's" scutum, too, until the end of the second century. The cavalry and the auxiliary infantry carried a six-sided shield.

The short lorica did not cover the stomach and thighs. To protect them, a wide belt was added to the legionary's armor. It was called the cingulum militari, or soldier's belt. It was made of leather covered with metal plates, and fastened with a buckle. Plates and buckle were usually made of silver. The end of the belt was split into four strips about six inches long. The top strip went through the buckle to fasten the belt. The four strips hung down to cover the stomach. They were studded with silver rivets. After a while, the strips were made separately and riveted to the back of the belt. Later still, a small iron plate was hung onto the belt and covered by the strips.

The sword belt and the cingulum militari were in each other's way, so the sword went back on a baldric. It was still worn on the right side, not in the Greek way on the left. A short dagger called a pugio was hung from the cingulum on the left hip.

Centurions and Praetorian Guards had a wider, richer cingulum, which had four rows of silver plates.

Before long, the cingulum militari came to have a special meaning to the legionaries. It was not just a piece of armor or a belt for his dagger. It was his badge, the mark of a soldier of Rome. When he took off his armor, he wore his belt with his civilian clothes so that everyone could see who he was.

The armor of the auxilia was always lighter than that of the legionaries. The infantry wore leather tunics and very wide leather shoulderpieces. Their helmets were made of leather, too. Archers, dartmen, and javelinmen wore little or no armor, of course. They wore leather or cloth caps and sometimes carried light shields of leather or wicker. They never got near the enemy if they could help it. They left that to the legionaries, who were better equipped for rough stuff.

Auxiliary cavalry wore their native armor.

The third century saw the end of the true legionary. Caracalla's law, which made all freemen Roman citizens, opened the army to men who just wanted a job and cheap food and clothes. They had no pride in being legionaries. None of them came from Rome. Many of them had been barbarians only a short time before. They were not disciplined and they were not tough. They wanted only to have as easy a time as they could.

They complained that the "gladiator's" scutum was too heavy. They were all given the light oval scutum. Next, they wanted a lighter helmet. They were given a simple iron pot, with rounded flaps hinged with leather for the neckguard and cheekpieces. Even this was too heavy. Leather helmets were tried next but they were no good either. By the fourth century, the legionaries wore no helmets at all.

The same sort of thing happened to the lorica. The lorica segmentata went first because it was the heaviest. Scale and mail followed soon after. Leather armor did not last much longer. By the fourth century, the new legionaries had no armor but their small round or oval shields. They wore long-sleeved linen tunics and long cloth breeches, bound below the knee with strips of ribbon or thong. They did not mean to march any more than they meant to fight, so, instead of the legionaries' hob-nailed sandals, they wore light shoes like slippers.

Their weapons were not the weapons of highly trained professional troops, as were the pilum and the Hispanic sword. These were deadly weapons in trained hands, but the new legionaries did not like training. Their weapons were a long sword and short javelins. The sword was called a spatha. It was a slashing weapon with a three-foot blade. Like all slashing weapons, it did not take much skill to use. Besides, the swordsman did not have to get too close to the enemy to use it. The new legionaries liked that idea.

The real pilum had been replaced by two new types of javelin: the spiculum or "sting," which was six feet long, and the vericulum, which was four feet long. These were ordinary javelins with wooden shafts and short iron heads. There was a heavy ball of lead just behind the head which made it easier to throw them straight. The new legionaries even used darts. These had lead shafts about nine inches long and barbed iron heads. The old legion-aries would have been horrified at the idea. They thought darts were barbarian weapons.

As the legionaries became more useless, the auxilia be-came more important. They were all barbarians, fighting for money. Nearly all of them were cavalry. They fought in their own way, not in the Roman way. And while the infantry wore less and less armor, the cavalry kept adding more and more to theirs. By the middle of the third century, both men and horses were covered in armor. They looked like iron statues.

Those that came from the West wore mail, since most of them were Gauls. They had long mail tunics with hoods that almost covered the face. Over the hoods, they wore round pot helmets with a cage that went over the face, like a baseball catcher's mask. Their legs were covered with breeches of mail. At the end of the third century, iron bands were added to cover the weak places at the elbows and knees, and even round the body, like the lorica segmentata. Cavalry from Eastern countries usually wore long scale tunics, padded breeches, and high, pointed helmets. With all this armor, they did not need shields. In any case, they needed both hands for their long, clumsy lances.

Many of the auxilia were archers, both on foot and on horseback. Unlike most archers, they wore heavy armor, like the mounted spearmen.

None of these men were Romans. They were not legionaries in the true sense. They fought for money, not for pride or as a duty to their City. The old legion and the spirit of the legion were gone. The power of Rome had gone, too. Europe was moving into the Dark Ages. With the end of the legions, the art of war moved into a Dark Ages of its own.

Frankish Knight, Eighth Century

4

The Age of Mail

The barbarians who had broken the Roman Empire swept over Europe. Visigoths and Ostrogoths, Bavarians and Burgundians, Vandals and Lombards, Franks and Teutons fought for land. Christians fought Moslems and Pagans. Huns fought everybody they met. Brother quarreled with brother, mother with son, uncle with nephew over the different kingdoms. For many centuries, Europe knew no peace. It was a Dark Age in history.

Then, very slowly, three great peoples grew up who were to shape the world of the Middle Ages. They were the Franks, the Vikings, and the Anglo-Saxons.

The Franks were one of the Gothic tribes who had been hired by the Roman Emperors to guard the borders of the Roman Empire. They had learned a great deal from the Romans. Even their language, French, came from the Latin spoken by the common people of the empire. In all the troubles of the Dark Ages, the Franks never quite lost their civilized ways.

When the Roman Empire fell, the Franks seized the lands they had been guarding, Gaul and Germany. In the fifth century, one of the leaders of the Franks, Clovis, brought all the different tribes of Franks together into one nation. For three hundred years after his death, the new Frankish nation went through many troubled times, but somehow it held together. In the eighth century, a strong ruler called Charles Martel or Charles the Hammer appeared. Under Charles and the rulers who followed him, the Franks became the greatest nation in Europe.

In the early days, the Franks were foot soldiers, while most of the other Goths were cavalrymen. Their troops had no armor except small, round wooden shields with iron rims and bosses, but they were huge men and fierce fighters. They wore their long blond hair in braids and had long mustaches. They used spears and long slashing swords, but their favorite weapon was a short-handled throwing axe, with a wicked curved head, which was called the *francisca* after them.

They also had long-handled battle-axes and a five-foot javelin. The javelin was thrown at the enemy's shield, not at his body. As soon as the head of the javelin was firmly stuck, the Frank rushed up and stamped on the shaft. This dragged the enemy's shield down or even tore it from his hand, so that the Frank could finish him off with a sword or battle-axe.

Frankish chieftains sometimes wore a helmet. These had long, shallow skullpieces and wide brims which turned up. They sat on the top of the head and left the sides of the head and the neck uncovered. The crown came to a point. Along the crown there was a flat crest shaped like the comb of a rooster or a fish's fin.

When Charles Martel became king, his first job was to throw out the Moorish Arabs who had taken Spain in 718 and were pushing into France. These Moors were mounted archers. They could ride rings around the Frankish foot soldiers and shoot them down from a safe distance. Charles needed cavalry to fight them. He knew that it took plenty of practice to learn to fight with a lance and shield on horseback, especially when his soldiers were not horsemen in the first place. His men had no time to practice, because when they were not fighting, they were busy tending their farms. So Charles freed them from work by giving them peasants to work their land while they were away learning how to fight on a horse.

Charles, though he probably did not know it, had started the second great Age of Cavalry and the Feudal System at one and the same time. In the centuries to come, these feudal knights became the most cruel, bloodthirsty and hateful rulers that Europe had ever known. However, right at the start, they seemed to be a good idea. The new Frankish knights smashed the Moors at Poitiers in 732 and saved Christendom.

The Frankish knights were heavily armored, to protect them from the Moorish arrows. They had wide, curved helmets which looked like turtle shells. A thick leather flap, called a hals-berge, or neck protector, hung from the back. They wore leather or cloth tunics with ring and scale armor. The scales were made of horn or leather, with square or leaf-shaped ends. The tunic came down to the knees and had sleeves to the elbow. The skirt was cut into wide strips to protect the rider's thighs.

The knights' shields were round or shaped like kites with round tops. They were made of wood covered with leather and bound with iron.

The knights used a twelve-foot lance and a huge slashing sword. The sword was worn on the left side, slung on a wide leather belt round the waist. The lance had become a deadly weapon, since Charles's knights had stirrups to push against when they thrust it home. The Moors had brought the stirrup into Europe. The Frankish knights were the first soldiers to use it against them.

Charles's grandson was one of the greatest men in history. He was the Emperor Charlemagne. Charlemagne added Germany and part of Italy to the Frankish kingdom. He invited many scholars and wise men to his court. France became the seat of learning in Europe and her scholars led the Western World out of the Dark Ages. There were many skilled craftsmen in France in Charlemagne's time. Not the least of these were the armorers. In their skilled hands, mail came back into use. It was to be the main type of armor for the next 450 years. This is what we call the Age of Mail.

Mail needed all the skill of a master craftsman. The iron wire could not be made in large amounts, because there were no machines to make it as there are today. Each piece had to be made slowly and painfully, by hand. A

piece of iron was hammered into a flat plate. This was cut into thin strips and each strip was hammered until it was round and thin enough to work with. The metal was hammered cold because this made the links much stronger. The strip was wound round an iron bar. When it was slipped off the bar, it looked like a spring. Each loop of the "spring" was snipped off. The ends of the loop were hammered flat and a hole was pinched or bored in each. The loop was then passed through the other loops of the mail, and fastened with a rivet which went through the holes in the ends of the loop.

It took a lot of patience and hard work and skill to make mail, but the effort was not wasted. Good mail would turn aside sword or spear without being damaged, and yet it would allow the knight to move and use his limbs freely.

Charlemagne's knights wore a waist-length coat of mail over a leather jerkin. The sleeves and bottom of the jerkin were scalloped.

They had two different kinds of helmet. The first looked like an iron derby hat. The second was a better type of "turtle shell" helmet. It had a rounder headpiece and a wide, sloping brim, which slanted out over the neck like a roof and curved up to make a pointed peak over the eyes. Both types of helmet had a heavy strip running across the crown for extra strength. The crest was riveted to this strip at the back. It was made of soft metal or leather and was usually shaped like a bunch of ivy leaves.

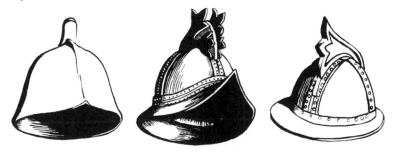

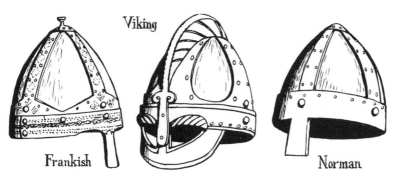

Viking

Frankish

Norman

In the tenth century, a conical helmet, shaped like a spinning top upside down, appeared. It was made of four curved triangles of iron welded and riveted to an iron frame, or simply riveted to each other. In the middle of the century, a short nasal was added. Sometimes a short neckguard was added too. The conical helmet replaced all other kinds of helmet for the next two hundred years.

During the tenth century, the hals-berge or neckflap was made of mail. Later it was added to the mail shirt and became a close-fitting hood which was called a coif. The name hals-berge or hauberk was then used for the whole mail shirt including the coif.

While all these things had been going on in France, the people of Scandinavia had been busy fighting among themselves. It was not until the end of the eighth century that they had time to look around and see what was happening in the rest of Europe. By the eighth century, their poor farmland could no longer provide them with enough food. Many Danes and Norwegians took to the sea for a living. This was called "going vicing," and the Norse sea rovers were called the Vikings.

They began to raid the rich countries to the south in their long "dragon ships." They attacked England, Ireland, and France, and later sailed right round Europe and into the Mediterranean Sea. Others sailed west and discovered Iceland and Greenland. In the year 1000, Leif Ericsson crossed the Atlantic and reached America (which he called Vinland, or the Land of Grapes) five hundred years before Columbus.

At first the Vikings had no armor, but when they started to raid the Franks, it became their favorite loot. By 850, the skilled smiths of the Norsemen had learned to make mail. From that time on, the Vikings wore mail shirts, which they called byrnies, and conical helmets. The helmet was made of iron or bronze plates, or had a frame of metal with horn or leather plates. Sometimes it also had a close-fitting neckguard and earflaps hanging on leather loops. A wild boar made of wood or bronze was used for a crest. (The horns and wings which are so often shown sprouting out of Viking helmets were very rarely seen in real life. The wings would have helped the Viking to run faster with the wind behind him, but otherwise they would not have been much use.) Chieftains sometimes added a metal faceguard, which came down to the chin. It had eyeholes and a mouth hole, and a bump for the nose with a metal mustache underneath it.

The Vikings carried large round shields made of two

Viking

thicknesses of wood and painted red. Their favorite weapon was the bow and they were skilled archers. Their bows were about four feet long with a string of reindeer sinew or braided strips of seal hide. They never lost their faith in the bow, and this played an important part in the history of armor, as we shall see later. But at that time they were the only archers in Europe.

They also carried long battle-axes and wide-bladed cut-and-thrust swords. Each Viking was proud of his sword and gave it a grim-sounding name, such as Leggbitr (leg biter), Kuernbit (millstone breaker), Skrofnung (gnawer), Nadr (viper), and Naegling (hole maker). (The names sound better in the Old Norse language than they do in English.) When a Viking died, his sword was broken so that no one else could use it. The pieces were buried with him so that he would have it when he reached the Heroes' Hall in Valhalla.

The Norse swordsmiths made their blades by twisting bundles of iron wires together and beating them flat. This left a wavery mark in the iron which is called "watering." It is the mark of a Viking blade. The swordsmiths also beat magic spells into the blades to make them more powerful. They cut the shapes of letters into the blade. Then they filled in the cuts with thin iron wire. The wire was hammered into the blade, which was then heated to fix the wire. Finally the letters were filed flat and the blade was polished. This is called inlaying. The spells were called runes. One rune in a blade found at Canwich Common, England, reads ANTANANANTANANTAN, and if that is not magic, I don't know what is.

When the Vikings landed on a raid, they would steal horses and rove across the countryside burning, looting, and killing. They always kept away from walled cities and fortresses because they did not know how to carry out a siege. The knights were the only soldiers well trained enough to beat the Vikings and well mounted enough to catch them. They were also the only men rich enough to build fortresses strong enough to keep out the Vikings. The common people of the countryside would drive their flocks inside the walls when the sea-rovers landed. Of course, they had to pay for the knights' protection by giving up more of their freedom. The Vikings helped to make the knights more powerful than ever before.

When Charlemagne died, his kingdom was divided among his three sons. At first they were too busy quarreling over it to deal with the Vikings. Then the Vikings attacked Paris, the chief city of France. Charles the Simple, who had been given France as his share of the kingdom, was finally forced to do something about them. So he hired Vikings to fight the Vikings. In 911, he gave a large piece of land at the mouth of the River Loire to a Viking leader called Rolf. In return, Rolf was to stop the raids on the French. Rolf and his men settled down to live there and the area was called the Northmen's land or Normandy. The leaders of the Normans soon picked up French habits and became feudal lords like the French knights.

The Angles and the Saxons lived in the north of Europe. About 450, Vortigern, the king of the Britons, asked the Saxon kings Hengist and Horsa to help him drive the Celts out of Britain. They did. Then they turned on the Britons and drove them out, too. Angles, Saxons, and Jutes poured across the North Sea to help in the fight. By the seventh century, Britain was ruled by the Anglo-Saxons and became the land of the Angles or England. The British had all been driven into the far north or into the country that is now called Wales. (King Arthur of the Round Table was one of the British chieftains who fought against the Anglo-Saxons. That is why the legends that sprung up about him first came from Wales. Later he became a great hero of the English. They had forgotten—or pretended not to remember—that he had fought against them in the first place.)

The Anglo-Saxons were foot soldiers. The only armor they had was small pointed leather caps like pixie hats and leather tunics. Their shields were round and small. They were made of a single layer of thin planks, with leather binding and an iron boss. Often they did not even use shields. Their favorite weapon was a mixture of a hatchet and a long dagger. It was called a seax. It had a wide, curved iron blade sharpened on one side. It looked a little like a machete. The Saxons were called after their weapon, seax-men, which became Saxons. They also used long spears with long, barbed heads. Like the Vikings, they were very proud of their swords. Unlike the Vikings, they passed them on from father to son. Atheling Athelstan left his brother the sword of King Offa, which had been passed on for over two hundred years.

When the Vikings began to raid England, Alfred the Great was king. He had no heavily armored horsemen to chase them with. Instead he built a navy to stop the arrival of more Vikings. Then he beat those that had already landed with his foot soldiers. For this reason the English remained foot soldiers until the Norman invasion. Even after that, infantry was never despised as it was in Europe and always played an important part in English armies.

The Anglo-Saxons learned to use conical helmets and mail byrnies from the Vikings. Still, not many used armor because it was very heavy for foot soldiers. They borrowed the huge, round shield, and the Viking battle-axe became their favorite weapon. One thing they did not learn from the Vikings was the use of the bow. This was a mistake, and they paid for it dearly at the Battle of Hastings.

In 1066, Duke William of Normandy claimed the throne of England. The English King Harold II refused to give it up, even though he had promised to help William to get it a few years before. That of course was before he unexpectedly became king himself. William landed on the south coast of England and Harold hurried south to meet him. The two armies clashed about ten

Norman Knight

miles from Hastings. (The battle is always called the Battle of Hastings. The place where it actually happened is called simply Battle to this day.) All day the English axemen and spearmen fought off the Normans from behind their shield wall. In the end, the showers of arrows from the Norman bowmen and the charges of the armored knights wore the English down. Harold himself was mortally wounded by an arrow. Under William, who was called William the Conqueror after that, England became a feudal state.

The armor of the Norman knights was the same as that worn by knights all over Europe in the eleventh century. It was to be used almost unchanged for the next hundred years. It consisted of a conical helmet, a mail hauberk, and a kite-shaped shield.

The helmet had a long, wide nasal, which completely covered the nose, and, sometimes, a short neckguard which came straight down the neck. Occasionally, it had leather earflaps. It was fastened under the chin with two thongs.

The hauberk reached the knees. The skirt was slit up the middle almost to the waist so that the knight could sit on his horse. The two flaps of the skirt were sometimes tied round the thighs with thongs so that they looked like short breeches. The coif covered the head except for a small facehole which left the eyes and nose and mouth showing. The facehole was split at the bottom so that the knight could pull the coif over his head.

The split was laced up tight and covered with a rectangular flap of mail fastened to the chest with studs. The hauberk's sleeves were wide and came down to the elbows.

Most hauberks were made of mail by this time. Some were made of ring armor. A few were made of scale. The scales were made of gaily painted horn or leather and shaped like leaves.

There were several different kinds of mail. The best kind was a fine mesh of riveted links. Each link was passed through the links around it before being closed, so that there were no holes for a point to slip through. Sometimes the links were fastened with two rivets; sometimes with rivets that had high pointed heads. This was called

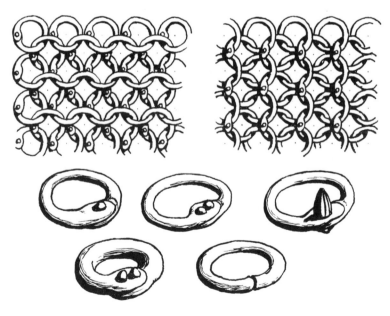

graine d'orgue, or barleycorn mail. Some mail had links twice as thick as ordinary mail, so it was called double mail.

Cheaper kinds of mail had welded links, or links which were closed but not fastened. The cheapest mail was made of links stamped or cut out of a thin metal plate. The cheap links were never used by themselves. There were always several rows of riveted mail between the rows of cheap mail.

Mail was very tiring to wear because it just hung on the body with nothing to hold it up. If you have ever been caught in a rainstorm wearing a heavy topcoat, you will have an idea of what it felt like. To stop it from dragging, it was tied with laces threaded through the links of the mail round the neck, the waist, and the tops of the arms. This also stopped the mail from chafing the knight's skin. The sword belt helped to hold the hauberk at the waist.

In the twelfth century, the knight wore a long, thickly padded tunic under his hauberk. It was needed to soften the force of a blow. Mail could not do this. It could save the knight from a lance point, but a thump from a mace would bruise him or break a bone. Even a soft blow could drive the links of mail into his skin, which made a painful wound. The tunic kept this from happening. It also helped to stop the chafing of the hauberk and soaked up the rusty stains which the mail had always made on his shirt. This must have made his laundress happy, at least.

The tunic was called a hacketon, which comes from the Arab word for cotton, *al-q̄utoun*. Cotton was often used for the padding. (The Crusaders brought cotton back from the East. They had to bring the Arabic name for it, too. As there were no proper rules for spelling words anyway in the Middle Ages, a word from another language made twice as much trouble. *Hacketon* is to be found spelled *acton, hacqueton, acketoun, aktun,* and about a dozen other ways. This is not so bad when you think that medieval people hardly ever spelled their own names the same way twice.)

Wool and old rags were used as well as cotton to stuff the hacketon. The padding was kept in place with quilting—that is, rows of stitches from top to bottom.

Some knights wore the hacketon over their hauberks. In this case, it was called a gambeson (which is sometimes spelled—in medieval fashion—*wambais*). The gambeson was covered with dyed silk and embroidered all over. Some poor knights wore it alone because they could not afford a hauberk. Other knights wore it instead of their hauberks because it was light and comfortable.

The knights' legs were not armored in the eleventh century. They wore cloth breeches and leather shoes. The breeches were often bound with cloth or leather strips. Sometimes the strips were covered with metal studs to give some protection to the legs.

The knight's shield was about five feet long so that it covered a mounted man from head to foot. It was made of

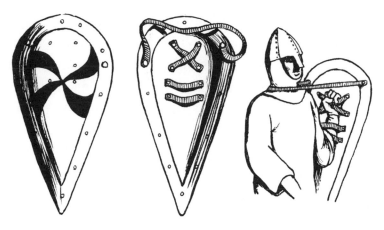

wood covered with leather, and it curved slightly. A long strap called a guige was riveted to the back. This went round the neck. Two small loops, called enarmes, went over the arm, so that the shield could be swung around to ward off blows. When the shield was not needed it was slung on the back by means of the guige.

The medieval people loved gay colors. The knights' shields were brightly painted with badges or with other eye-pleasing designs. (They had to be repainted after each battle. It was a good thing the knight had someone else to do his work for him.)

The main weapons of the knight were the lance and the sword. The lance was a simple spear about ten feet long with an iron head. The shaft was made of ash wood which was very strong but springy. The springiness took the shock of the blow out of the shaft. A stiff shaft would have been torn out of the knight's hand when it struck. Later, the knights learned to couch their lances. This means that the lance went under the armpit and was locked in place by the arm. The forearm ran along the shaft to hold it even more firmly. A couched lance could be aimed better, and the whole weight of the knight and his horse were behind the thrust instead of just the weight of his arm.

The knight's sword had a blade about three feet long. The blade was sharpened on both edges and had a blunt point. The sword was used as a slashing weapon because there was no point in stabbing at a man in mail. The hilts were straight and long, and the pommel was a round knob.

The sword was carried in a leather-covered wooden scabbard. It hung straight down on the left side. The scabbard was carried on a wide leather sword belt. The belt was fastened in an odd way. One end was split into two long strips; the other had two slots cut in it, one above the other. The strips were pushed through these slots and knotted on the other side.

The mace was another common weapon. Usually it was simply a wooden club about three feet long. Better maces had an iron head shaped like the club in a deck of cards. The mace was carried at the saddle bow to be used if the knight lost or broke his sword in the middle of a battle. It was the favorite weapon of fighting clergymen—and there were plenty of them in the Middle Ages. (Bishop Odo of Bayeux was one of the Norman leaders at the Battle of Hastings. The famous Bayeux Tapestry, which tells the story of the battle, was made at his command.)

Clergymen used the mace because they were forbidden to shed blood. The mace did not shed blood: it cracked skulls and broke bones.

The hauberk became longer in the early part of the twelfth century. It reached down to the ankles. This was done to give the legs better protection, but it made the hauberk too heavy and clumsy. By 1130, it was back to its old length.

About the same time, the sleeves of the hauberk became longer and tighter. They were brought to the wrist, where they were tied with a drawstring. The older, wide sleeves were comfortable, but a lance could easily slide up the opening and wound the arm or shoulder. Later in the century, the sleeves were made even longer so that they covered the hands like mittens with a separate thumb-piece. A hole was left in the palm of the mitten so that the knight could free his hand by slipping it through the hole and pushing the mitten back on his wrist.

A drawstring was added to the coif. It was threaded round the temples and tied at the back. Another was threaded round the facehole. These stopped the coif chafing the knight's face and scalp by holding the coif firmly in place.

To give the face more cover, a flap called a ventail was attached to the side of the facehole. It was wrapped around the chin and throat, and tied or buckled to the drawstring. The knight could easily unfasten it to get a breath of fresh air or to let cool air into his hauberk.

For a time, the scabbard was worn underneath the hauberk. The top poked through a slit on the left hip. This was done so that the sword belt would not be cut through by a lucky blow. It was a clumsy idea and was soon given up, because a better way of hanging the scabbard had been found. It was held by two thin belts which hung from the wide waist belt. The ends of these thin belts were braided around the scabbard and tied. Instead of hanging straight down, the scabbard could be hung at an angle by making the front scabbard belt longer than the back. This made it easier to draw the sword and kept the scabbard from tangling with the knight's feet.

The sword changed little in the twelfth century. The hilts were curved up, which made it easier to catch an enemy's blade and turn it aside. Pommels were the shape of a fig or a Brazil nut. The lance had not changed at all but by 1130 the knights had learned to couch them.

The greatest change in twelfth-century armor took place in the helmet. The conical helmet became taller and the top became rounder. The nasal got longer and wider. Then it spread out and became a faceguard which covered the whole face. A slit, called a sight, was cut in the top of the faceguard for the knight to see through, and holes, called vents, were cut in the bottom so he could breathe.

Suddenly, at the end of the twelfth century, the round-topped helmet was replaced by a flat-topped iron hat. It had shallow sides like a cake tin and a faceguard. This usually had a bar running up the middle to make it

  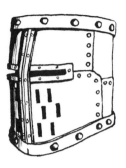

stronger. At the beginning of the thirteenth century, a short neckguard was added to the helmet. This quickly became wider and so did the faceguard. About 1215, they met in the middle. The knight's helmet had become a helm which covered his head completely. It was called a pot helm because it looked like a cooking pot without a handle. Some pot helms had sides that bulged out like a barrel, and this type is called—strangely enough—a barrel helm.

Pot helms and barrel helms sat right on the top of the knight's head. The flat top gave no sort of glancing surface, so, to stop his skull from cracking every time he was hit on the helm, the knight had to wear an iron skullcap

and a padded cap underneath. The padded cap, which was made out of canvas or leather, was called an arming coif. It was worn under the coif of the hauberk. It was kept in place by two wide strips of cloth which were tied under the chin. These also helped to keep the mail of the coif off the face. The iron skullcap went under the mail coif and sat on top of the arming coif.

About 1150, the front of the legs and the top of the feet were covered with long strips of mail about three inches wide. They were buckled to the girdle of the breeches and tied round the leg with leather thongs. Toward the end of the century, the mail strips were replaced with mail tights called chausses, which completely covered the legs. The chausses were held up in the same way as the strips. To stop them from scraping the knees and dragging, they were tied just below the knee with a drawstring or with a wide strip of cloth.

The knight was now covered with mail from the top of his head to the soles of his feet.

At the beginning of the thirteenth century, the knights began to wear a long linen robe over their hauberks. It was called a surcoat. The surcoat came down below the knees, sometimes as far as the ankles. It had no collar or sleeves. It was split right up the sides and laced up from the waist to the armpit. The long skirts fell free, and were split up the middle like the hauberk. The sword belt was worn around the surcoat to hold it in at the waist.

There is a mystery about where the surcoat came from

Crusader, about 1225

and what it was for. Some experts claim it was first worn by the Crusaders to stop the Mediterranean sun from making their mail red hot. But the knights wore it whether the sun was shining or not. They went on wearing it when they came back to Europe where the sun is never very hot. Anyway, stuffed inside their gambesons and hauberks and chausses and pot helmets, they were probably so hot that the weather outside made very little difference. Other experts say the surcoat was to keep the rain from making their mail rusty. But mail had been worn for a long time and nobody seems to have been bothered by the rust. In any case, the knight always had someone else to clean his mail for him. (This was done by rolling it about in a barrel filled with sand and vinegar.) Besides, even if the surcoat was made of waterproof material, the neck and armholes were too wide to stop the rainwater from trickling down inside.

The most likely idea is that the surcoat was used to show off the knight's coat-of-arms.

About the time the surcoat first appeared, the face-guard came into use. No one could tell who was behind it because it completely covered the face. The knights began to use badges on their shields so that everybody would know who they were. Each knight had his own special design which no one else could use. It was called a blazon or coat-of-arms. The king's heralds kept a record of each blazon on great rolls of parchment. The coat-of-arms was passed from father to son. Some noble families in Europe today still use the design that appeared on their ancestor's shield 750 years ago.

The knights were very fussy about being mistaken for someone else so they plastered their coats-of-arms all over everything: their castles, their swords, their banners, their followers' tunics, their horse's harness, even their wife's dresses and of course their shields. The surcoat meant that they could show it off in a bigger, better, and brighter way.

So that there was not the smallest chance of a mistake's being made, each knight had his own special crest too. This was usually an animal or bird. It was made of parchment, wood, and leather. Most crests were huge things anywhere up to three feet high. The crest became part of the coat-of-arms, and was drawn over it on the herald's rolls. Today many people use the word *crest* when they mean a coat-of-arms. This is quite wrong.

All the very strict rules about what colors and designs can be used, and where they should go, and which coat-of-arms belongs to whom, is called heraldry, after the king's officers who used to keep the rolls.

The knight's horse was given a surcoat just like his master's. A tight hood covered his head and neck except for his muzzle, his ears, and his eyes. A long cloth which swept down to the ground covered his body. The horse's surcoat was called a trapper. Of course the trapper was smothered with his master's coat-of-arms, too.

Toward the middle of the thirteenth century, the top

of the pot helm became rounder to give a glancing surface. The iron skullcap began to slope down to cover the
ears and the neck. This type of skullcap was called a
bascinet, or little basin. Because the pot helm was so heavy,
many knights left it off and fought in their bascinets,
which were then worn over the coif.

Another type of open helmet came into use at the same
time. It usually took the shape of a cowboy's hat with a
rounded headpiece and a very wide, straight brim. It was
called a kettle hat because it was shaped like an old-
fashioned cooking pot or kettle. Some kettle hats had
pointed crowns; in others, the brims slanted down. Kettle
hats were very popular helmets and were used until about
1500. Common soldiers used them frequently, especially
archers.

The knights wore special underwear which could stand
up to the tearing and rubbing of the mail. It was a tough
cotton material like corduroy called fustian. The name
came from the old name for Cairo in Egypt, El-Fustāt.
(The knights brought back from the Crusades many

Arabic words like *fustian* and *hacketon*.) Hacketons were often made of fustian. The knights also wore many pieces of padded fustian to soften blows and to stop the chafing of mail.

When the knight armed for battle, he first put on his ordinary underwear, a linen shirt and breeches. Then he drew padded fustian breeches over his legs and tied them at the waist. The mail chausses were pulled on and tied or buckled to the breech girdle. Then a padded roll called a bolster was tied round the waist. This took some of the weight of the hauberk off the hips. The hacketon with heavily padded shoulders was pulled over the head. The hauberk was put on over the hacketon and the drawstrings pulled tight and tied. The surcoat came next. After the sides had been laced up, the sword belt was knotted round the waist and the sword checked to make sure it was hanging comfortably. The arming coif was tied in place and the bascinet was pushed on firmly. Then the mail coif was pulled up and tied over them. The ventail was wrapped around the chin and buckled. The pot helm was hung at his shoulder and his shield round his neck.

And, in all this, the knight was still supposed to be able to leap into the saddle without using his hands.

Longbowman

5

The Age of Change

The longbow and the crossbow brought the Age of Mail to an end. Mail could turn aside a sword blade but it could not keep out arrows and crossbow bolts. The armorers set out to find a new kind of armor that would. They began adding steel plates to the mail. For 150 years, as bows became more powerful and bowmen more skilled, they were forced to keep adding more plates: plates to plates, and plates on top of plates. By the time they had finished, they had the knight covered in plate armor from head to foot. They won the battle against the bowmen, but, as we shall see, they won it too late.

This period, roughly from 1250 to 1400, is sometimes called the Age of Mixed Armor because plate and mail were mixed together. A better name would be the Age of

Mixed-up Armor. The armorers did not seem to know what they were doing at times. Many strange ideas were dreamed up and then thrown out. The knights themselves made things even worse than they might have been. They hated change of any kind. Many of them still hung on to their mail long after the others had changed. In England, they always seemed to be years behind. It is sometimes very difficult to make out just what was happening and when it was happening in the Age of Mixed-up Armor.

One thing is *not* difficult to understand, and that is the reason why the longbow of the English yeomen began the change from mail to plate.

The English found the longbow in Wales. They were amazed at what the Welsh archers could do with their longbows. A knight's horse was wounded by an arrow after it had gone through the rider's hauberk, his leg, and the saddle. At the siege of Abergavenny Castle, the Welshmen shot their arrows right through an oak door nearly two inches thick. After this, the English kings hired Welsh bowmen to fight in their armies. By the fourteenth century, the English had learned how to handle the longbow themselves. From that time on, longbowmen were always the largest part of every English army.

English longbows were made of yew wood with a hemp or silk string. So many bows were made in the Middle Ages that yew wood became scarce. Laws had to be made which forbade anyone to sell bows abroad.

Merchants had to bring in yew bowstaves with every cargo of goods or wine. No one under the age of seventeen could use a yew bow, and bowyers had to make four bows of some other wood for every one of yew. Even to this day, the yew tree is rarely found growing wild in the English countryside.

The bowstave was over six feet long. It could send an arrow about three hundred yards. The shaft of the arrow was of wood. The head was a pointed steel cap on the end of the shaft. The flights were usually made of brightly colored goose feathers or of gay peacock feathers. It was often called a cloth-yard shaft because it was as long as the distance from the end of the arm to the ear. This was used by weavers and cloth merchants as a rough yard measure for their goods. They held the cloth at their chin with their right hand and drew it through their fingers with their left hand until their left arm was stretched straight out.

The bowman drew his bow in the same way. He stood with his left side to the target, and held the bow in his left hand with his arm stretched straight out from the shoulder. He drew the string back to his right ear with the tips of the first three fingers of his right hand. The arrow was fitted to the string by means of a small notch cut in the end of the shaft. This was called the nock. The arrow was held steady between the first and second fingers, and its head lay on the left hand against the left side of the stave.

The bowmen wore very little armor. They trusted to their bows to keep the enemy away. A good bowman could shoot between twelve and fifteen well-aimed arrows a minute. Even heavily armored knights thought twice before charging through a hail of arrows like that. The only armor the bowmen wore was a leather jacket and an iron skullcap. A few wore coifs or collars of mail which they had picked up from dead knights on the field of battle. They wore wide leather belts in which they carried their shafts. On their left wrists, they had a leather or bone wristguard to protect them from the lash of the bowstring. They also carried a sword or dagger. When they had used up their arrows, they would creep in among the struggling mounted men, wounding horses and finishing off the knights who had fallen.

The only way to become a good bowman was to start at an early age. The Englishman was given his first bow when he was six or seven years old. As he grew bigger and stronger, he was given bigger and stronger bows, until at last he was able to use the true six-foot longbow. Even when he was grown up, he was kept at practice. One law, passed in 1441, said he had to spend all his spare time at archery practice instead of playing football or handball or quoits. He could be fined for practicing at a target which was less than 220 yards away. Every parish in the country was bound to send a number of bowmen to the army when the king called for them, and to see that they had spare bowstaves and strings and plenty of arrows.

The king could use them for forty days free of charge. After that he had to pay them or send them home. In 1238, an archer from Chetton Manor had to serve until a slab of bacon he had brought with him had all been eaten. I imagine he had bacon for breakfast, lunch, dinner, and supper.

The longbow was a powerful weapon. It could pierce mail and wooden shields. But it could not pierce plate armor unless a lucky arrow found a chink between the plates. When the knights began to wear plate, the long-bowmen began to shoot at their horses; this was as good as killing the rider. When the knight was thrown from his saddle, he was usually stunned by the fall and occasionally broke his neck. In any case, in sixty pounds of armor it was difficult for him to get back on his feet without help. French knights gave up riding into battle when they were fighting the English. They left their horses behind and walked. By the time they reached the English line, they were usually too tired to do any serious fighting. At the Battle of Agincourt in 1415, they had to tramp nearly a mile across rain-soaked fields to reach Henry V's tiny army. Five thousand French noblemen died in the mud that day and a thousand more were taken prisoner. Nobody bothered to count the number of common soldiers who fell. The English lost thirteen men-at-arms and about one hundred other men. (At least, that is what they claimed.)

While the English kings were doing everything they

could to make the English yeomen into first-class archers, the noblemen of the rest of Europe were doing everything to stop their peasants from becoming skilled with weapons. They were afraid of rebellion, because they ruled more harshly than the English noblemen did.

European armies had to hire mercenary troops. Their archers came from Italy, and the best of them came from the city of Genoa.

Their weapon was the crossbow.

The crossbow or arbalest appeared about the same time as the longbow. The Crusaders may have found it in the East and brought it back to Europe, or it may have grown out of the small catapult bows of the Romans. (The name arbalest comes from the Latin *arcus ballista*, or catapult bow.)

It was so deadly that Pope Innocent II banned it in 1139. He said it was "deathly and hateful to God." However, the Crusaders were allowed to use it against the Saracens because they were heathens. When Richard the Lion-Hearted came back to Europe, he decided to arm his troops with it, whatever the Pope had said. So he had no one to blame but himself when he was killed by a crossbow bolt while besieging an unimportant baron who had defied him. Before long, everyone had followed Richard's example—in using the crossbow, that is, not in being killed by it.

The earliest crossbows were made of a thick curved piece of wood about two feet long. Later they were made

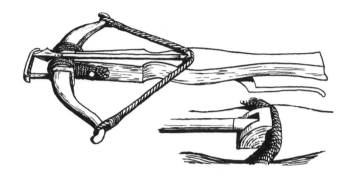

of strips of horn or whalebone glued together between two layers of wood and bound round with sinew. Finally, in the fourteenth century, they were made of steel. The bow was tied across the end of a wooden bar called the stock. The steel bows had to be kept in place more firmly so they were fitted into a slot in the end of the stock as well. The string of the bow was made of many strands of waxed twine, twisted or braided to make a rope about half an inch thick. A small roller called the nut was sunk into the stock about halfway along. It had two hooks on top which caught and held the bowstring when it was pulled back. On the bottom, there was a notch. The trigger, which went through the stock, fitted into the notch and held the nut steady when the string was caught on the hooks. The bolt went into a groove in the top of the stock with its end resting against the string. When the trigger was pulled, it let go of the nut, the string was jerked off the hooks by the pull of the bow, and the bolt was fired.

This may seem a complicated way to fire a bow. However, it meant that a man could use a crossbow without much training. All he had to do was to drop a bolt in the slot, point the bow at the target, and pull the trigger. Learning to use a longbow, on the other hand, took about twelve years of steady practice.

The crossbow fired a dart called a bolt or quarrel. (It is never called an arrow.) It had a wooden shaft about a foot long, and a short steel head. Sometimes it had flights made of leather; sometimes it had no flights at all. One type of bolt, called a vireton, which means twister, had long flights which curved round the shaft like the stripes on a candy cane. These made the bolt spin in the air, which sent it farther than straight flights. The name *quarrel* came from the Italian word *quadrelli*, or four-sided. Quarrels had square heads while the ordinary bolt had a flat, leaf-shaped head.

The early crossbows were loaded by pulling the string back with the hands. The whalebone bows and the steel bows were too strong for that. All sorts of contraptions had to be invented for loading them: hooked levers, windlasses and winches, ropes and pulleys, cogwheels and ratchets, and many others. The crossbowman had to cart one of these loaders around with him wherever he went. Even so, the crossbow was hard to load. It could be fired only about three times a minute. (The French knights, who were always ready for a fight, sometimes could not wait for their slow crossbowmen to get into action and simply rode right over them.) However, while the cross-bow lacked in speed, it was very powerful. It could out-shoot the longbow by more than a hundred yards and could pierce all but the best plate armor at short range.

At first, the knights were too stubborn to see that they needed something stronger than mail to protect them from cloth-yard shafts and quarrels. They hated a change even if it was for their own good. In any case, they thought that bows were cowardly and unfair, and did not want anything to do with them. They wanted to go on fighting in the old way, where a battle was a sort of game played by mounted men in armor. They could not believe that a commoner fighting on foot could beat a nobleman fighting on horseback. They clung to this idea while the bow-men knocked more and more of them out of their saddles.

At last they had to give in. Now they went too far the other way. They used horn, whalebone, leather, cuir-bouilli, cloth, iron, steel, brass, and latten (a hard mixture of brass and other metals) to make large plates, and small plates, and splints, and scales. Plates and padding and mail were piled on top of one another. But after fifty years of this the armorers had learned the new craft of working with steel plates. They began to make sense of the ter-rible mess. From 1350 on, they were busy perfecting plate armor, and by 1400 the great age of the armorer had begun.

Studying this period is difficult because so many dif-ferent things were going on at once and many of them do not seem to make much sense. In addition, each piece of armor had its own special name, and many pieces had more than one name. To make things even harder, the men who wrote about armor were as mixed up as the armor. They often used different names for the same thing and the same name to mean entirely different things. For instance, the word *vambrace* was sometimes used for all the armor on the arm, and sometimes for just the armor on the forearm. The armor on the upper arm was then called the rerebrace. But rerebrace was also used for all the armor on the top of the arm and the shoulder; or just the armor on the upper arm (and the shoulder armor was called a spaudler); or just the armor for the shoulder, when the armor on the arm was called a vambrace. To mix things up completely, the word *brassarts* was also used for the armor on the arm.

So that we know what we are talking about, only one set of words will be used in this chapter and the next, and we will forget about all the other words we could use instead of them. The other words will be put in a list at the end of the next chapter, because you will find them used in other books on armor and on fighting in the Middle Ages, and also in museums. Many of these words were not used by the men who wore the armor; they were invented by armor collectors and writers on armor in the nineteenth century, who sometimes had pretty funny ideas about armor anyway. I'll point out in the list which are the true words and which are the made-up ones.

The first plate that the knights wore goes back to the twelfth century. It was the plastron or chestpiece, which was worn under the hauberk. After the surcoat appeared, the plastron was worn over the hauberk and under the surcoat. In the early thirteenth century, it was replaced by a better defense, called the cuirie. The cuirie was a breastplate of cuirbouilli. Before long, a backplate was added to it. The two plates were buckled together at the shoulders and waist. The word *cuirie* comes from the French word *cuir*, leather. In England, it was sometimes called curace. From this we get the word *cuirass*, which is used for a body defense made up of a breastplate and backplate, whether it is made of leather or not.

The first plate to appear in the open was a defense for the knee, called the knee cop. To start with, it was a small, round plate, riveted to the mail over the knee. It kept getting larger, and by 1270 it began to curve round the sides of the knee. By this time it was fastened to the leg by laces threaded through the mail, or by a strap which went round the back of the leg. It was squarer than the earlier knee cop. Occasionally it also appeared in the shape of a maple leaf or a four-pointed star.

Toward the end of the thirteenth century, the knee cops were riveted to thigh defenses called cuisses. These were padded leggings of fustian or leather which looked like waders cut off just below the knees. They were strapped or laced tightly over the chausses at the knee and held up by strings tied to the girdle of the breeches.

About 1260, shinguards called schynbaldes were added to the leg harness. They looked like drainpipes cut in half. They were tied to the chausses or fastened over the chausses with straps and buckles. Like most plate armor of the thirteenth century, both the schynbaldes and the knee cops were made of cuirbouilli. It was not until the end of the century that they were made of iron.

The only armor to appear on the arm before 1300 was a small disc over the elbow. This was known as a couter, from the French word *coude*, meaning elbow. Couters first appeared about 1260. Like the first knee cops, they were tied to the mail, and like the knee cops they grew steadily larger. By the end of the century, the couters had become curved and covered most of the point of the elbow.

The legs were covered with plate, not because of arrows but because a foot soldier could get at a mounted man's legs easily. It was not quite so easy to reach his head and body. Nothing much was added to the arms because the knight wanted to be able to swing his sword or mace freely.

A strange piece of harness appeared about 1270. It was the ailette, which means a little wing. Thirteenth-century writers mention the ailette but they never bothered to say what it was made of or what it was for. Ailettes were tied to the top of the arms, with most of them sticking up above the shoulder. They came in all sorts of shapes—rectangles, ovals, discs, diamonds, fans, and shields. They were about nine inches high. They were made of leather or buckram, a stiff cloth like canvas, with a coat-of-arms painted or embroidered on them. They could hardly have been armor because they were not solid enough, they were not firmly fastened, and they could not have protected anything anyway tied to the outside of the arms. The coat-of-arms may be the answer to the mystery. Ailettes appeared at about the same time that the knights' faces were being covered by the faceguards of the pot helm, and disappeared when the open bascinet became popular about 1340. From the side the blazon on the shield and the surcoat could not be seen, but the ailettes would have solved this problem. Besides, the knights loved any kind of colorful decoration.

Some changes were made in the hauberk. The coif became a separate piece, which was given a new name, cap-of-mail, or camail for short. It fitted tightly round the head and throat, including the chin and often covering the mouth as well. A slit had to be cut in the back of the neck so that it could be pulled over the head. When it was in place, the slit was fastened with a lace. A stiff collar of double mail was added to the neck of the hauberk.

About 1250, mittens with separate fingers were tried out but they never caught on. In any case, the mittens were replaced by gauntlets at the beginning of the fourteenth century. These were made of leather and lined with canvas. They were stiffened with small plates and strips of whalebone. The knuckles and the joints of the fingers were covered with thick, pointed knobs called gadlings, or little spikes. The gadlings made the gauntlet into a deadly weapon. The knight did not bother about fair play or gentlemanly behavior when he was fighting. He used his spiked fists, his elbows, his feet, his shield, and anything else that was handy. He would not have been allowed into a modern boxing ring, though he might have been at home in a hockey game.

Several improvements were made on the flat-topped helm. The top began to curve up to a point in the middle

 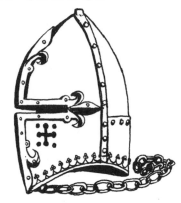

and then became rounded. The sides curved in toward
the top. By the end of the thirteenth century the helm
had taken on the shape of a beehive. The sides grew down
until they reached the shoulders. This was known as a
great helm. It was better than the pot helm in many ways.
The curved, pointed top was a good glancing surface,
the shoulders took the weight instead of the top of the
head, and there was more room inside. It sat more firmly
on the head than the pot helm. The inside was lined with
a leather cap, riveted to the sides of the helm. The top of
the cap was loose and could be pulled tight with a drawstring like the mouth of a sack, to fit tightly over the head.
Even if the great helm was knocked off, it could not fall
to the ground because it was hooked to the belt by a long
chain which was stapled to the inside of the faceguard.

The iron skullcap was still worn under the helm. However, more knights were beginning to use their skullcaps
instead of helms. Their motto seemed to be comfort before safety.

An extremely important part of the knight's equipment during the thirteenth century was not a piece of armor: it was the spur. The spur became the mark of the knight and a badge of his nobility. Spurs were needed only by a man who rode a horse, and the only people who rode horses were the nobility. The most important day in a young nobleman's life was the day he received his spurs and became a knight. It was even more exciting if he was knighted for bravery in battle. This was true even for a king. During the Battle of Crécy, King Edward III's son, the Black Prince, was fighting so far ahead of the English line that his men were afraid that he would be cut off by the French. They sent a messenger to the king to ask for help. The king refused, saying, "Let the boy win his spurs." The Black Prince won his spurs that day and became one of the great heroes of England.

The first spurs were short spikes called prickspurs. They were attached to a small round plate riveted to the heel of the chausses. After 1250, the spikes became longer. They were mounted on a U-shaped metal strip which fitted round the heel and was strapped round the foot.

About 1320 the rowel spur took the place of the prick-spur. The rowel was a wheel of spikes. It was attached to a forked iron rod by a pin in the same way that a wheel is fixed on a wheelbarrow. When the knights were fighting on foot, they took off their rowel spurs, which were just in the way, and used them as caltrops. Caltrops were small iron balls with four spikes sticking out of them. They were scattered on the ground to make the enemy's horses stumble. (The word *caltrop* means heel catcher.) Rowel spurs made good caltrops if there were no proper ones handy.

The knight's sword hardly changed from 1200 to about 1280. It had a wider, shorter blade than the twelfth-century sword, with a narrow groove running about half-way down the blade. It might be a good idea to explain the groove once and for all. Many people have the idea that the groove was put in the blade to stop it from sticking in a wound or to drain off the blood, though they do not seem very clear about how this happened. Both ideas are nonsense. The groove was put in the blade partly to keep down the weight of the sword and partly to give some spring to the blade. The lance was made of ash wood for the same reason. If the sword blade had had no spring to it, the sword would have been torn out of the knight's hand with the shock of a solid blow on an iron helm. Try hitting a rock with an iron bar and you will get an idea of what it would have felt like.

The thirteenth-century sword had a sharp point, although it was still used mostly as a slashing weapon. The hilts thickened at the ends and in some cases were shaped like a bowtie. They also began to slant or curve up toward the blade. The pommels were shaped like discs or like wheels with spokes.

About 1280, a shorter, wider-bladed sword appeared, mostly in Italy and Spain. The blade narrowed to a sharp point and the hilts curved sharply. This type of sword was a thrusting weapon. In the north of Europe, a massive sword appeared at about the same time. It was called an *épée de guerre* or war sword. It had a narrow, pointed blade between thirty-six and forty inches long and a handle over six inches long. It was also called a hand-and-a-half sword because sometimes the first two fingers of the left hand were hooked around the handle to steady it while the right hand swung it.

Swordmakers were beginning to stamp their trademarks on their work. The best blades came from Passau in Germany and carried the mark of a running wolf or a unicorn. In place of the runes of the Viking swords, short prayers or religious phrases were inlaid in the blade. The most popular was "In Nomine Domini" which means "In the Name of the Lord." The phrases got longer and longer until only the first letter of each word was used. Odd things like NEDRCNEDRUSDRCNEDRUI, which looks more like a pagan spell than anything else, began to appear. If it had been spelled out, the sword would have needed a blade nearer six feet long than three, but at least we might have been able to find out what NEDRCNEDRUS-DRCNEDRUI stood for.

A single-edged slashing sword called a falchion appeared in the thirteenth century. This was nothing more than a large seax, although its name came from the French word for a sickle, *fauchon*. Like the seax, it had a wide blade with a curved cutting edge.

The knightly sword belt with its metal decorations was usually fastened with a buckle after 1250. The scabbard

was hung differently. The sword belt ended in a loop which went round the top of the scabbard. The belt buckle was attached to a short strap which split into two at the end. One of the ends of the buckle strap was woven through slits in the belt close to the loop. The other was wound round the scabbard and the two ends were tied together. The long end of the belt was either draped over the scabbard or simply left hanging down in front.

The knight carried a spare short sword, called an estoc, or thruster, at his saddle bow. This had a wide blade

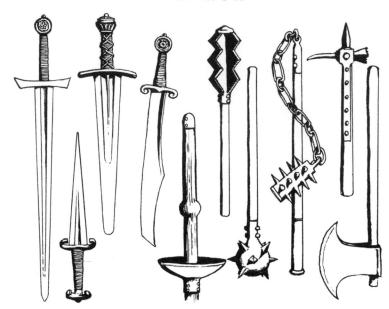

which narrowed to a point, and could be used if the war sword was dropped or knocked out of the knight's hand. Sometimes a broad-bladed dagger called an anelace was used instead of the estoc.

The lance had not changed at all, but in the last part of the thirteenth century a handguard, called a vamplate, was added to it. The vamplate was shaped like a pot lid about six inches across. The lance went through the middle of it. The vamplate was riveted to the shaft about two feet from the end. It not only guarded the knight's hand, it stopped the hand from slipping when the lance was thrust home.

Some old weapons had been improved and some new ones had appeared. The mace had become a much better weapon. It had an iron shaft and an iron head, covered with knobs or spikes. One kind of mace had a round head with long spikes sticking out all over it like the rays of the sun. The knights, who had a strange sense of humor, called it a *Morganstern,* or morning star. Another clubbing weapon like the mace was the war hammer, which was sometimes called a *bec de fauchon,* or hawk's beak, because it had a thick curved spike on the back. The spike was used to pierce mail or was slipped through the sights of the helm. It could also be used as a hook to drag the enemy off his horse. The battle-axe appeared again. A long-handled type, like the Viking axe, was used for fighting on foot; a shorter one was used on horseback. Finally, there was a horrible new weapon called the military flail. The flail was one of the farm tools which the peasants often used in battle. It was used to thresh corn and made a handy sort of club. The military flail was an iron ball attached by a long chain to a wooden handle. One type had an iron bar covered with spikes instead of a ball. It was called a holy water sprinkler. It usually sprinkled more blood and brains than holy water. The military flail was the favorite weapon of King John of Bohemia, who was blind. He used to ride into battle laying about him on all sides. With a flail, you did not have to see your enemy to hit him; you simply swung it around you until it struck something. Unfortunately, he seems to have hit his own men who were leading his horse as often as he hit an enemy.

The knight of 1300 still looked the same as the knight of 1200. The cuirie and the cuisses were hidden under the long surcoat and hauberk. A few knights wore schynbaldes and gauntlets but these were not widely used until after 1300. The differences that could be seen were the great helm, the ailettes, and the knee cops. Also, more knights were wearing skullcaps and kettle hats.

After 1300, the knight's appearance began to change quickly. New pieces of armor were added. Older types were changed and improved, or simply disappeared.

Schynbaldes became popular. About 1320 a second plate, covering the back of the leg, was attached to the schynbalde by hinges. The two plates made a tube which completely covered the leg below the knee. They were fastened together by straps and buckles on the inside of the leg, so that they could not be cut by accident. This type of leg armor is called a closed greave, or simply a greave.

The knee cop began to curve round the sides of the knee and sometimes went right around the leg. It had wide, flat borders with thick rims. The edges were often decorated with strips of latten cut into spikes or leaves or fleurs-de-lys. Sometimes a strip with decorated edges on both sides ran from top to bottom of the knee cop.

Strips of whalebone, and later of metal, were riveted into the lining of the cuisses. The heads of the rivets were usually gilded. The cuisses were also covered with silk

Knight, about 1300

or velvet. Cuisses of plate first appeared about 1320, but few knights wore them until after 1350.

A plate defense for the foot also appeared about 1320. It was called a sabaton from the French word *savate*, meaning a boot. To start with, the sabaton was made of small plates riveted to a strip of leather which ran down the instep. By 1340, the plates curved right round the top of the foot like a shoe. The sabatons were fastened on with laces which ran round the bottom of the foot.

The year 1320 was a big one for plate armor. The rest of the vambrace was added to the couter or elbowpiece that year. One plate, the upper vambrace, covered the outside of the top of the arm; another covered the top

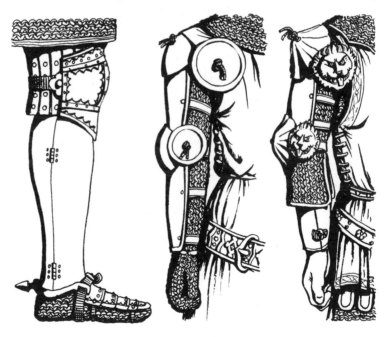

of the forearm. The couter became larger. It covered the gap between the upper and lower vambrace and began to curve round the arm. The three plates of the vambrace were tied to the sleeves of the hauberk with leather laces.

A second plate covering the inside of the arm was added to the lower vambrace about 1325 and to the upper vambrace about 1340. Like the plates of the greaves, they were hinged on the outside and fastened with straps and buckles on the inside out of harm's way. Sometimes the lower vambrace was worn under the sleeve of the hauberk, which had to be split to the elbow so that the plates would fit under it.

A small, round shoulderpiece called a spaudler first appeared about 1300 and became popular by about 1330. When the ailette disappeared, the spaudler was tied to the sleeve of the hauberk in its place.

There were still two gaps in the vambrace, one at the armpit and one at the bend of the arm. These were covered with small discs called besagews, which were also tied to the mail. The word *besagew* is another of the mysteries of the age of change. It is the English way of pronouncing *bisaigüe*, the French name for the Frankish double axe. I cannot imagine why a small metal disc should be called after that fearsome weapon, but it was.

The knight's armor was becoming decorative as well as useful. Besides the embroidered, gold-studded cuisses and the fancy borders of the knee cops, the besagews were sometimes shaped like lions' faces and the spaudlers had curlicued edges. The plates of the vambrace and the greaves were being shaped to the curves of the arm and the calf. Now that the armorers were becoming skilled in working with plate, they were beginning to think about what their handiwork looked like. Unfortunately, in the first half of the fourteenth century, the knight did not look at all beautiful, or romantic, or even warlike. His arms and legs looked trim enough, but everywhere else he sagged and bulged like an old sack.

His body armor was now in four thick layers of plate and padding and mail.

Over everything was the surcoat. This was now padded like the hacketon. Sometimes small, rectangular plates were riveted into the padding down the front, as far as the waist. It was covered with rich material and the coat-of-arms, made of patches of colored cloth and silk or gold thread, was embroidered on the front and back.

About 1325, throughout most of Europe, the skirt of the surcoat was cut off just below the hips to give more freedom to the legs. In England, only the front of the skirt was cut off, leaving the back hanging down behind. Why this was done is hard to say. Perhaps the English knights liked their surcoats so much that they could not bear to part with them. Like somebody getting into a cold bath, they had to do it a little at a time. By 1340, the English had caught up with everyone else.

The new short surcoat was called a jupon after the Arabic *jubba*, which was a sort of long padded waistcoat.

It fitted tightly to the body down to the waist and then became a short loose skirt. It was usually fastened at the back with buttons or a lace. By 1350, the skirt was tight-fitting too, and the jupon followed the lines of the knight's body.

Underneath the surcoat came some sort of plate, unless the surcoat of plates was worn. The cuirie was still popular and, after 1300, often had iron plates riveted to it. Another type of plate came into use at the end of the thirteenth century. This was the coat-of-plates.

The coat-of-plates was a thigh-length leather tunic, with iron plates riveted inside the lining. It looked like a long life jacket and it was put on in the same way. The head went through a hole in the middle so that the coat hung down in front and behind. The front had flaps on each side which wrapped round the body under the arms and buckled together at the back. The chest and back and

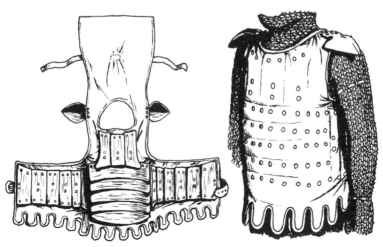

sides were covered by long, narrow plates running up and down. Three or four plates ran from side to side across the stomach. The coat was often covered with silk or velvet, and the hem was scalloped. The rivets holding the plates were usually filed into ornamental shapes. Like the cuirie, the coat-of-plates was worn over the hauberk.

The skirt of the hauberk was not needed once the legs were covered with plate. First, the sides were cut away, and the front and back were left hanging down in a long point. After 1325, the points were cut off too. The short hauberk was called a haubergeon, which means little hauberk. The sleeves of the haubergeon came about halfway down the forearm, and, as we have seen, they were often split to take the lower vambrace. The hacketon of course was the same length as the haubergeon.

During the fourteenth century, the bascinet quickly became the most popular helmet. By 1350, it had replaced the helm. The helm became tournament armor after that.

The sides of the bascinet grew down and covered the ears and the top of the neck. The sides sometimes slanted back from the face, and sometimes came straight down and covered the cheeks as well. The top of the bascinet became taller and the sides curved in to a point like the great helm.

The camail lost its top and became a sort of mail curtain, riveted to the rim of the bascinet and hanging down to the shoulders. About 1330, it was fastened differently so that it could be taken off and replaced easily. A row of

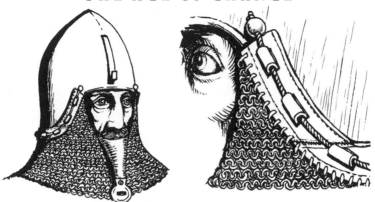

small staples called vervelles were attached to the bascinet. They ran round the bottom and up the sides of the facehole. Matching holes were made along the top of the camail so that it could be hung onto the staples. A lace or wire passed through the staples kept it in place. The bottom of the camail was tied to the surcoat with a lace or fastened with a strap and buckle, back and front. This stopped it from flying about when the knight moved his head.

A nasal made of a flap of mail attached to the bottom of the camail's facehole appeared about 1310. It was replaced with a solid metal nasal by 1340. The nasal was pulled up over the face and hooked onto a stud on the front of the bascinet. Neither kind of nasal was stiff enough to do much good, but a real visor did not appear until 1360.

Toward the middle of the century, a new piece of plate appeared. This was the gorget, or throatguard, a high collar which covered the throat and curved up around the chin. It fastened at the back of the neck with a strap, and was worn with the kettle hat or occasionally with the bascinet.

The common soldiers at this time still had only leather or padded tunics. The lucky ones added a small cape of mail called a tippet. A few had kettle hats or iron skull-caps, but most of them went into battle bareheaded or with cloth hoods on their heads. Shields were hardly ever used, even by the knights. Crossbowmen sheltered behind a huge wooden shield while they reloaded their bows. These shields were called pavises, after the Italian city of Pavia where they were invented. Longbowmen stood behind a hedge of sharpened stakes and kept the enemy off with a storm of arrows.

Most of the other foot soldiers were armed with one of the new pole weapons. The most famous of these was the halberd, invented by the Swiss about 1300. The head of the halberd had an axe blade on one side, a hook for pulling mounted men out of their saddles on the other, and a spearhead on top. It was fixed onto the end of a thick nine-foot shaft. The Swiss Guard in Vatican City are still armed with halberds. Most of the other pole weapons had a mixture of spear blades, spikes, hammers, and hooks, too, and every one had its own name. We still have the weapons and we know all the names, but no one is quite sure which weapon goes with which name.

After 1300, the armorers had solved all of their problems with plate armor but one: they could not make iron plates bend and stretch. Then someone did solve the problem, but no one knows who he was, where he lived, or even just when he found the answer. He was the man who invented the sliding rivet.

Usually, when two plates were to be riveted together, a hole just wide enough to take the rivet was bored through them. The rivet was pushed through the hole and hammered flat on the inside. With the sliding rivet, a slot was cut into the lower plate instead of a hole. A washer was placed over the slot, and the rivet was pushed through the hole in the top plate, the slot in the lower

plate, and the washer. The end was then hammered flat on the inside of the washer. The top plate could slide over the bottom plate as far as the rivet could slide up and down in the slot. (You can make a sliding rivet for yourself, but use two pieces of cardboard and a brass paper fastener. They are easier to work with than iron plates and rivets.)

These sliding plates are called articulated plates, from the Latin word *articulatus*, which means jointed. When articulated plates were curved slightly, they could bend and stretch with a joint such as the shoulder. When the arm was raised, the plates slid back over one another;

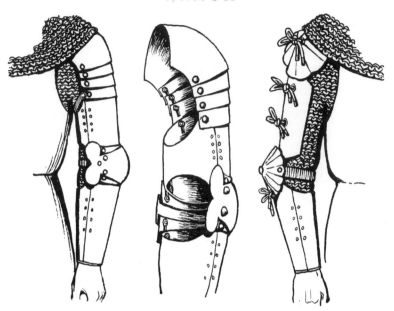

when the arm was lowered, they stretched out again, just like a concertina. Of course articulated plates were not new—lobsters had been wearing them for centuries.

Articulated vambraces began to appear about 1340. The upper and lower vambraces were attached to the couter with three or four narrow plates called lames, from another Latin word, *lamina*, which means a thin shell. The spaudler became a curved plate covering the shoulder. It was strapped under the arm and was joined to the vambrace with three or four articulated lames running down the arm. The articulated vambrace was called the Italian vambrace, for no particular reason. Perhaps it was named in honor of the Italian armorers who were already becoming famous for their skilled work.

The Italian vambrace never caught on with the Germans until long after 1400. They went on tying the plates to the sleeves of the haubergeon. Perhaps they were just being stubborn, or perhaps they could not get their tongues round a word like *articulated*.

After 1350, padded cuisses began to disappear and plate cuisses took their place. They were fastened round the thighs with straps and buckles and held up by strings tied to the girdle of the breeches. The cuisses were never closed unless the knight was fighting on foot. If he had worn closed cuisses on horseback, he would not have been able to keep his seat. Smooth steel is not the best thing for keeping a tight grip on a saddle. However, a long plate was hinged to the outside edge of the cuisse about 1390, to cover the gap on the side of the thigh between the cuisse and the saddle.

The knee cop and the cuisse were joined together by one or two articulated lames. The greave was fastened to the knee cop by another type of fastening called a turning pin. This was a small metal pin shaped like the letter T which stood up on top of the greave and which could

Knight, about 1350

turn right round like a little turnstile. The turning pin went through a slot cut in a lame attached to the bottom of the knee cop. When it was given a half turn, the arms of the T caught on the sides of the slot, but still allowed the lame to move up and down.

By the second half of the thirteenth century, the armorers had not only learned to make plate bend and stretch, they had also learned a lot about shaping it. They became artists in steel. The plates of the vambrace and of the leg harness became curved so that they fitted snugly to the shape of the limbs. The knee cop and couter were made smaller and more cup-shaped so that they fitted better over the knee and elbow. The sides were lengthened into wings that stood straight out behind to cover the important tendons in the bend of the arm and behind the knee. The ends of the wings were shaped into circles or ovals at first, and later, as the armorers became confident enough to decorate their work, into heart shapes. The small plates of the sabatons were held together with sliding rivets and were cleverly curved to follow the shape of the foot. The gauntlets were made of plate, too. One large plate was shaped to fit over the back of the hand and make a wide cuff, shaped like a bell. Tiny plates were riveted to the leather fingers of the glove.

But the best example of the armorers' skill was the bascinet. The bascinet started off as a single lump of iron. Using only a hammer, the armorer shaped it into a graceful helmet.

Toward the end of the century, the shape of the bascinet changed. The point began to move backward. By
1380, the point was right over the neck. The back of the
bascinet went straight down to the nape of the neck, and
the front slanted sharply down to the forehead.

About 1360, bascinets with visors began to appear. At
first the visor was a small flat plate which covered only
the facehole of the camail. It was attached to the bascinet
by a hinged bar. The bar fitted over the studs that had

been used to fasten the nasal. By about 1370, visors had
become larger and were attached to the helmet by rivets
on the sides. By 1380 they covered the whole face and
curved round over the edges of the bascinet's facehole.
The middle was pushed out to a point to make room for
the knight's nose. Above the "nose" of the visor were
two slots for the eyes, and underneath was a longer slot
for a breathing hole. After a while, the "nose" became
longer and turned into a long, pointed snout. The bascinet

now looked like a wolf's head. The sights above the snout looked like slanted eyes, the vent underneath looked like a snarling mouth full of teeth, and the small round vents on the snout looked like whiskers. It gave the knight a fierce and sinister look, which is always helpful in a fight. The Germans called this kind of helmet a *Hundsgugel*, or hound's cap. This was too fanciful for the English; they called it a pig-faced bascinet. (They could not pronounce *Hundsgugel* anyway. They called it Hounskull.)

By 1370, the camail had grown large enough to cover the shoulders. The string and staples which held it to the bascinet were covered with a strip of metal which hooked over the camail. Just above this, an ornamental gold strip called a fillet ran around the bascinet. Different kinds of fillets showed the knight's rank. Kings and princes wore small crowns. Barons and other high noblemen had fillets decorated with strawberry leaves. Sometimes, instead of a fillet, the knight wore a padded roll of cloth like a turban. This was called an orle. At first it had been used as padding when the bascinet had been worn under the great helm.

Now it was worn as decoration, covered in rich cloth, embroidered and studded with small pearls and precious stones.

The camail had grown larger until it hung down to the shoulders and curved down over the top of the chest and the back. A gorget, or throatpiece, was probably worn underneath it. About 1390, the camail disappeared and the gorget was used by itself. It took on the shape of the camail, something like a baby's bib. From this it took the name beaver, which comes from the French word *bavière*, meaning a bib. The top of the beaver jutted out like the bow of a ship so that it covered the chin. Until about 1400, the beaver was held on with a strap round the neck, like the gorget. After that it was riveted to the sides of the bascinet. When the visor was pulled down, it fitted over the top of the beaver so that there was no gap. Another plate was added which curved round the back of the neck and was riveted to the beaver at the sides, so that the knight's neck was completely covered with steel plate.

While the arms and legs and head were being covered with solid plate, the body armor was changing too. After 1350, the haubergeon, the coat-of-plates, and the jupon were made even shorter, so that they just covered the hips. The jupon was usually lined with silk and covered in brightly-colored velvet, with the coat-of-arms embroidered on the front and back. The hem was scalloped or cut into a fringe of clover leaves or fleurs-de-lys.

The cuirie and the surcoat of plates had almost completely disappeared by 1375. Meanwhile, the armorers were working on the coat-of-plates. They turned it into two completely different kinds of body defense. One was a light armor, where the plates became smaller and smaller and more of them were used. The other turned into the solid plate cuirass as the plates grew larger and larger and finally joined together to make one big plate.

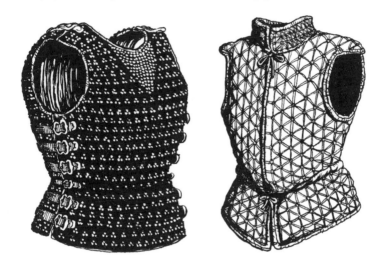

The light armor was called a brigandine. It was a padded linen tunic covered with velvet. It came down to the hips, and fitted tightly to the knight's body. The plates of the brigandine were about two inches long and one inch wide. They were riveted in overlapping rows inside the lining of the brigandine, so that the rivet heads showed on the outside. Thousands of plates and rivets went into every brigandine. One made for the king of Spain had nearly 4,000 plates and over 200,000 rivets.

Because of its handsome appearance and gay colors, the brigandine was most popular in Italy. Because it was light, it was popular with foot soldiers. Most of them wore a cheaper kind of brigandine called a jack. This was made of small square plates which were sewn into the lining of a coarse cloth tunic. The word *jack* come from the French for James—*Jacques*—which was the slang word for just anybody in the Middle Ages, as we use John Doe for an ordinary man nowadays. The name *brigandine* came from the French word *brigand*. In the Middle Ages, this simply meant a foot soldier. It came to mean a bandit later on, because the common soldiers, or brigands, were not paid very often, so they took to stealing their food in order to live. Once they found out how easy it was for an armed man to take what he wanted, they began to take other things as well as food. Wandering gangs of brigands roamed the countryside when there was no fighting. They robbed the farmers, drove off their cattle, and burned their barns. So far as the poor country folk could see, there was very little difference between soldiers and bandits, so they used the same name for both.

The solid cuirass was made from the chest plates of the coat-of-plates, which became larger and finally joined together. First, there were five or six narrow plates, then two large plates, and finally, by about 1365, a single large plate which covered the whole of the chest. The same thing happened to the backplates, but it took a little longer. However, by 1375, the knight had a solid curved cuirass, which came to the waist. It was held together by several straps up each side and over the shoulders. The stomach plates did not grow into a single plate like the breast and backplates. Instead they became longer and more curved until the front and backplates met at the sides. They were fastened together with straps and buckles. This skirt of steel hoops was called a fauld or a paunce. (*Paunce* is the same as *paunch*.)

The cover of the coat-of-plates had disappeared by this time, but the plates were still riveted to a leather tunic. About 1390, the final improvement was made. The plates of the cuirass and the fauld were hinged together on the right-hand side instead of being buckled. This made it easier to put on and was a safer fastening than leather straps, which could be cut in a fight. The plates of the fauld were riveted to straps fastened to the bottom of the cuirass. This meant that the body armor held itself up instead of having to be fastened to a tunic. The leather was glued to each plate, separately, as a lining. The knight now had a full suit of plate from head to foot.

The great moment had at last arrived. As the fifteenth century began, the knights got rid of their jupons. The gay colors of velvet and gold thread gave way to the cold glint and gleam of steel. The Age of Plate had begun.

Milanese Armor,
about 1420

6

The Age of Plate

The last and greatest period in the story of armor began just after 1400. It lasted less than two hundred years. By the middle of the sixteenth century, the Age of Plate, the Age of the Feudal Nobleman, and the Age of Armor had all come to an end together.

In a way, the noblemen brought their own end on themselves. They opened up a new world when they went Crusading to the Holy Land. The new ideas and new things they brought back to Europe upset the careful balance of the feudal world and knocked them off their high perch.

For themselves, they brought back new ideas about stone castles to replace their wooden ones and about new siege catapults to knock them down again. But they also brought back cloves and cinnamon, lemons and melons, sugar and silk, cotton and glass mirrors, and new dyes. Where the Crusaders had gone to fight, merchants followed to buy and sell. Great trading cities sprang up along the routes to the East. Like the polis of Ancient Greece each one made its own laws, coined its own money, fought its own wars, and paid respect to no man.

To fight their wars, the cities hired armies of mercenaries who were called "free companies." In Italy they were called condottieri, and they became something of a joke. The condottieri could see no reason for risking their necks while the merchants sat safely at home. They fought their battles like games of chess and rarely got down to real fighting. In fact, sometimes the captains of the two "enemy" armies would get together before a battle and agree to put on a show for their employers. When they had made enough noise to satisfy their employers, they called it a draw before anyone was hurt. At one such battle, at Zagonara in 1424, the only men killed were a condottieri captain and two of his followers who fell off their horses and drowned in a muddy ditch. Not all mercenaries were like the condottieri however. Most of them fought hard when they were paid regularly. And they always fought to win because they were not paid if they lost.

The trouble with mercenary troops was that they did not go home quietly when the war was over. They waited around for the next war to begin. While they were waiting, they kept themselves by robbing and looting the countryside. In order to free their countries from these brigands, the kings of England and France and Germany started full-time professional armies. These royal armies were the policemen of the Middle Ages. They were made up of specially picked commoners, trained and armed like the knights, who were called men-at-arms. (In French, this is *gens d'armes*, and the French call their police *gendarmes* to this day.) Once the mercenaries had been dealt with, the kings found they had full-time armies for their wars.

The wealth of the merchants had helped the kings to put their unruly nobles in their place. In return for this help, the kings began to use common men as ministers and advisors. The power of the noblemen began to slip away, and a new air of freedom blew into the feudal world. The common folk, once they had felt this freedom, were ready to fight for it. They formed their own citizen armies. When the noblemen tried to stop them, they found they had something more than untrained peasants to deal with.

In 1305, the men of Courtrai beat an army of French knights after trapping them in a bog. The French knights would not fight until it was too late because the townsmen were not gentlemen. The men of Courtrai were not so fussy. (They were armed with a strange spiked club called a *Godendag,* which means "Good day!" It was anything but a good day for the knights.) In 1315, the Swiss let the French knights ride into a narrow valley near the town of Morgaten, then cut them to pieces with their halberds. Later, the Swiss exchanged their halberds for long pikes and became the most efficient troops in Europe. They proved many times that well-trained infantry could beat armored horsemen if they refused to fight the knights' way.

War was becoming a job for the professional, not a sort of game for a nobleman who had nothing better to do. The knights' idea of fighting for its own sake was disappearing. The mercenary fought to win because he had to. The professional soldier fought to win because it was his job. The citizen armies fought to win because their freedom depended on it. All three used anything that came to hand and all three were willing to try something new if it helped them to win. One of the new things that they tried was the gun. And guns, more than anything else, brought the Age of Armor to an end.

Guns first appeared at the beginning of the fourteenth century, but we do not know who invented them or how they were invented. Gunpowder had already been known for a long time. The Chinese had been using it for centuries in fireworks and rockets. However, the first time anyone talked about gunpowder as an explosive was when the English scholar Roger Bacon wrote in 1249 that it could be used to blow up castle walls. Even he did not realize that it could be used in a gun. So some unknown genius made the first gun some time between 1250 and 1300.

It was simply an iron bucket, half filled with powder and topped up with rocks. A slight improvement on this, at the beginning of the fourteenth century, was the fire pot. This looked like a brass flower vase with a round belly and a long neck. (In fact, the Italians called them *vasi*.) It fired a large iron quarrel. Real cannon appeared about 1320. The word *cannon* comes from the Greek word *canna* meaning a reed or hollow tube. That is what the early cannon was, an iron tube.

It was usually made by the local blacksmith. He took long strips of iron, often made out of old horseshoe nails, and fastened them round a thick pole or round beam. Then he closed up the cracks between them with his hammer. Next he heated iron rings and slipped them over the strips. When the rings cooled, they shrank and bound the strips more tightly together. The whole thing was then heated in the furnace until the wooden beam was burned away. This iron tube was called a barrel because it was made of strips and hoops like a beer barrel. We still use the same word today.

Forged cannons were made in all sizes. The biggest ones were called bombards. In the fifteenth century, there was a fashion for gigantic bombards. One was made for King James II of Scotland in 1463. It was called "Mons Meg." The barrel was thirteen feet long and weighed five tons. It was made in two parts so that it could be moved about. It fired an 1,100-pound iron ball nearly a mile, and needed 105 pounds of powder to set it off. (King

James became even more famous as the first king to be killed by a gun. He was standing too near a cannon when it blew up.)

By the middle of the fifteenth century, cannon barrels were being cast in molds, which was quicker and less expensive than forging. The bellmakers made the first cast barrels because they were used to handling large molds. They often melted down bells to get the brass or bronze they needed. They made two molds, one for the inside or bore and the other for the outside of the barrel. The molds were made of clay and baked hard. Then they were hung on a high wooden frame, one inside the other, and rocks and earth were piled up around them to keep them from cracking. Then the metal was melted and poured into the space between them. When it had cooled, the barrel was taken out, scraped, and polished, and was ready to use.

The barrel was tied or chained down to a bed of heavy wooden beams. Large wooden stakes were driven into the ground behind it to stop the gun from kicking back when it was fired. Cast barrels were no trouble to load. The powder and ball were poured into the mouth, or muzzle, and jammed down tight with a long pole called a ramrod or drivell. With a forged barrel, it was not so easy. Gunpowder will explode only if it is set off in a tightly closed space. Otherwise, the gases, which build up and make the explosion, seep out and the powder merely

fizzles like a damp firecracker. The gunmakers tried fitting a plug in one end of the barrel, but it was blown out every time the gun went off. Then the breech was invented.

This was an iron tube with a carrying handle, about the size and shape of a large beer stein. It held the charge of gunpowder. At one end was a small nozzle which fitted into the bore of the cannon. The breech was jammed in between the barrel and the stakes and wedged tight. With any luck, it would stay put when the cannon was fired.

Much later, breeches were made which screwed into the barrel. Breech-loading iron cannon were used until the sixteenth century. After that, they disappeared until the middle of the nineteenth.

In the top of the barrel or the breech there was a small hole called the touchhole. This was filled with powder called priming powder. When a flame was touched to the priming powder, it shot through the touchhole and set off the charge. At least the gunner hoped it would.

Medieval gunpowder was not very good. The mixture that was used—four parts of saltpeter and three parts each of charcoal and sulphur—was not the best explosive mixture and the chemicals were not very pure. They were ground together until the powder was a fine dust. If the gunner packed this powder too tightly, the gun did not fire at all. If he packed it too loosely, the gunpowder burned instead of exploding and the cannonball barely made it out of the barrel. And even if he used exactly the same amount of powder each time, the gun might shoot under or over the target. If he was really unlucky, the gun blew up and killed him and his crew.

Cannon were so untrustworthy that they were only used for sieges until the end of the sixteenth century. A castle or a town was big enough for the gunner to stand a chance of hitting something when and if his gun went off. However, the cannon were good enough to take away the knight's stronghold. He could not hole up in his castle and thumb his nose at his enemies once the cannon balls started to tumble the walls and towers around his ears. At the end of the fifteenth century, guns were mounted on proper carriages pulled by horses. (Until then, they had been hauled slowly from place to place on their wooden beds by oxen.) The French King Charles VIII was the first to use these field guns in open battle. Even so, at the battle of Fornovo in 1497, only ten of the thirty-five hundred men who died were killed by gunfire.

Hand guns appeared in the first half of the fourteenth century. At first they were simply small cannon fastened to the end of a pike handle with metal bands. They had a range of about one hundred yards, but the hand gunner was lucky if he hit anything at forty yards. It took him about two minutes to load his clumsy weapon, and after five or six shots he had to stop and scrape the crust of burned powder out of the barrel. However, hand guns were improved much more quickly than the cannon were.

The handle or stock was shortened and the barrel was fastened along the top. The touchhole was moved to the side of the barrel, where the wind could not blow the powder out and the rain could not soak it. A small cup called the pan was placed underneath the touchhole to hold the powder. Until 1400, a red-hot wire was used to fire the priming powder. In the fifteenth century it was replaced by a slowly smoldering length of rope which was called a slow match. This meant that the hand gunner did not have to stay close to an open fire in order to re-heat the wire. (It also meant that the cannoneers were no longer blown up while mixing their powder near the fire.)

The new hand guns were much lighter and better made. They could be held against the gunner's chest and aimed better. They even had a hook on the bottom so that they could be steadied on the top of a wall. From this, they took the name *arquebus*, which is French for hook gun. Even with these improvements, it still took two hands to hold the gun and an extra hand to hold the slow match. Three-handed gunners were not easy to find so something else had to be done.

The "something else" was the matchlock or serpentine. This was an S-shaped lever pivoted in the middle on the side of the gunstock. The top held the match in a loop; the bottom curled under the stock like a trigger. When the trigger was pulled back, the serpentine swung round and brought the match down to the touchhole. This could be done by the fingers of the right hand while both hands held the gun and aimed it.

The arquebus became a dangerous weapon. It had a range of two hundred yards and a good marksman could

hit a playing card at half that distance. More important, it was powerful enough to pierce plate armor at forty yards.

In the sixteenth century, a huge arquebus called a musket appeared. It was invented in Spain. (Musket comes from *moschetto*, the Spanish word for falcon.) The musket was twice as powerful as the ordinary arquebus. It was just as easy to use because the stock was curved down at the end, rather like the butt of a modern rifle, to take away the tremendous kick of the gun. It weighed up to forty pounds and had a six-foot barrel. The end of it had to be propped up on a metal stake with a forked top. The musket had a range of four hundred yards, because of its long barrel, and could pierce armor at over a hundred. It was the weapon that finally beat the armorer. He could make a suit of armor that would stop a musket ball, but it was so heavy that a man could not move about in it.

This was the last straw for the knight. Fighting had been taken over by professional soldiers. Politics had been taken over by the middle-class merchants. His castle could be blown to pieces by cannon, and now he had to give up his armor. The world had changed around him while he had stood still, and there was no place for him.

There was no place for the armorer either, but at the end of the Age of Plate he could look back on a century and a half of glory. For it was during this period that the armorer became the king of the craftsmen. He had learned his craft from the fumbling and mistakes in the Age of Change. He had learned it well. The suit of plate that the armorers came up with was as good as armor could be. It was the model for all the work done in the Age of Plate. It is surprising how little difference there is between armor made at the beginning of the fifteenth century and armor made at the end of the sixteenth, when the Age of Armor, was coming to an end.

What changed most were the shapes of the different plates. The armorer had solved the problem of protecting the knight. Now, like all craftsmen, he wanted to show that he was an artist as well as a good workman. Different styles of armor developed, just as different styles of painting or writing do.

Two countries, Italy and Germany, led all the rest. Armor made elsewhere was usually a copy of the Italian or German styles. The Italians liked plump, rounded shapes with curved edges and smooth surfaces; the Germans liked slimmer, straighter lines with spiked or pointed edges. The difference between the two styles is really the difference between the way the Italian and the German people look. After all, plate armor had to follow closely the shape of the man who wore it.

In addition to the great styles of armor, there were fashions in armor, just as there are fashions in clothes. The German style led to a fashion called Gothic armor, which was popular in the last half of the fifteenth century. Gothic armor went out of fashion about 1500 and was replaced by Maximilian armor. This in turn gave way to a highly decorated fashion called Pisan armor.

There were national fashions too. Italians wore colorful brigandines or covered their armor with velvet; Germans preferred "blued" armor; the French and the English liked the gleam of naked steel. Different countries liked different types of helmet. Armor even followed the fashions of everyday clothes. Sabatons made with long, pointed toes, called pikes, imitated the ridiculous fashion of making the toes of men's shoes so long that they had to be tied up to the knees. In the sixteenth century, men's outer clothing was made with loose, puffy, padded lines, and covered with slits, or slashes as they were called, to show the rich cloth of the shirts and breeches underneath. Bulging, puffy armor was made to look like the clothes.

Finally, the different sizes and shapes that men come in had a lot to do with the way their armor looked. Armor could not be altered like clothes. It had to fit perfectly or it was no use. Besides, each knight had his own pet ideas about what his armor should look like and how it should be made. The Emperor Maximilian wrote to his armorer, Conrad Seusenhofer, "Make my armor the way I want it because I am going to have to fight in the tournament in it, not you." It was a good point, and since he was paying for it you can be sure he got his way.

Many of the changes, then, were due to changes of fashion or of taste. Others were made because of the need for greater strength, or to make armor more comfortable.

Guns did not begin to play a big part in warfare until the sixteenth century. The weapons the armorer had to deal with in the fifteenth century were still the lance, the sword, and the crossbow. (The longbow was still an important weapon but was not a real danger to the knight himself. The crossbow, on the other hand, was an armor-piercing weapon.)

The lance had grown much longer and heavier. The shaft thickened up to the vamplate and narrowed off to a point at the end. Just behind the vamplate it was cut down to make a grip for the hand. The sword became a cut-and-thrust weapon with a narrow blade. After 1425, rings were added to either side of the hilt. They were called finger rings or pas d'ane—that is, donkey's hoofs—from their oval shape. The first finger was hooked around the ring for thrusting. It helped the knight to steady and aim the sword, and to fence with it. Hacking away at plate armor did very little harm: the knights had to learn to thrust at the cracks between the plates.

For hacking they used a falchion, a battle-axe, a war hammer, or a mace. When they fought on foot, they used a pole-axe, which was a short halberd with an axe blade, a hammer, and a spearhead. Daggers were popular. A new dagger called a main-gauche, or left-handed dagger, was used to block the enemy's sword when the knights were fencing. The sword and dagger were worn on a narrow, jeweled hip belt, or carried in metal loops riveted onto the fauld.

Shields were no use against the heavier lances, and were hardly ever used after 1400 except in the tournament. In any case, the knights had learned to cross their lance over to the left side of their horse's neck so that their own left side was turned to the enemy. This made a much smaller target. Boxers nowadays fight with their left side turned to their opponent for the same reason.

The fifteenth-century armorers found two ways to deal with the new lance and the new way of fighting with it. One was to strengthen the armor, especially on the left side; the other was to make more and better glancing surfaces.

The Italians led the way in strengthening armor. In Italian suits, many of the plates were made larger and more small plates or lames were used to join plates together. In this way, the small gaps that had been protected only by the mail of the haubergeon were covered with plate.

The pauldrons grew down to overlap the breastplate and cover the gap at the armpit. The bottom of the right

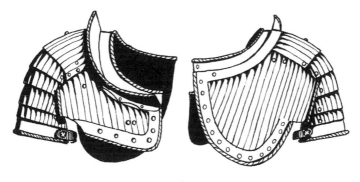

pauldron had to be cut away so that the lance could be couched under the arm. By the end of the fifteenth century, the pauldrons had spread so widely at the back that they overlapped. The edges had to be trimmed straight down to stop them from jamming together and pinning the knight's arms to his sides.

The wings of the couters and knee cops were made larger and were curved around the gaps at the bend of the arm and behind the knee. Toward the end of the century, they were often made without wings. Instead, the sides went right around and joined at the back. In the sixteenth century, small couters and knee cops with wings came back, and the gaps were filled with small articulated plates.

The gap between the fauld and the leg harness was covered with a pair of plates, called tassets, hanging from each side of the fauld. These were really the bottom strip of the fauld split into two pieces. About 1420 a curved piece had been cut out of the bottom of the fauld so that it would fit over the saddle. The tassets were the two pieces left. They were hung onto the fauld with straps and buckles. They became rectangular and then triangular or shield-shaped. By 1450 they were long enough to overlap the top of the cuisses. A little earlier, small tassets were added at the sides and a long plate, called a rumpguard, to the back of the skirt. Tassets were called after the purse or pouch which men hung at their belt in place of a pocket. (The knights liked to show off their legs

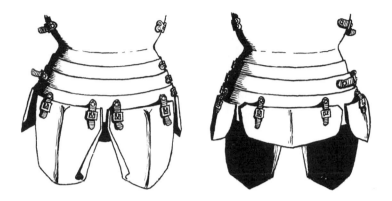

so they wore their hose as tight as possible and there was no room for pockets.)

The gorget or throatguard came back as a new piece of armor to cover the gap between the bottom of the helmet and the cuirass. It had two large plates which overlapped the cuirass and ran up to the bottom of the neck. Two or three curved lames were riveted to the top and fitted round the throat. The back and front of the gorget were held together on the right side with a loose rivet which worked like a hinge, and fastened on the left with a turning pin.

Besides making the plates larger, the Italian armorers also made them thicker on the left side and added extra plates, called double or reinforcing plates, so that parts of the armor had two layers of steel. A double plate called the gardbrace or arm guard was fastened on the front of each pauldron with a staple and pin. The staple was attached to the pauldron and went through a hole in the

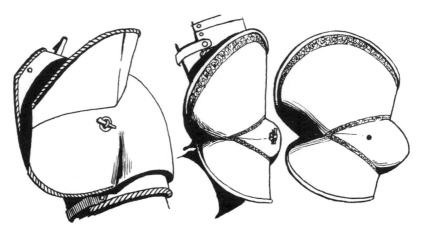

gardbrace. The pin was wedged into it on the outside. On the left side, the gardbrace covered the front of the pauldron up to the top of the shoulder.

Another double plate was fastened to the couter. It was called the guard of the vambrace. It was the same shape as the couter but much bigger. It had large wings that spread out over the upper vambrace and overlapped the lower vambrace. Double plates were also riveted to the front of the helmet, the wings of the couter and the knee cop, and the tops of the cuisses.

The smooth, curved plates of the Italian style of armor were excellent glancing surfaces. However, because they were so rounded, the lance was likely to slip off in any direction into a gap in the armor. To prevent this, thick rims were added to most of the plates. Some plates were bent up at the edges, or "turned." Turns were made at the top of the breastplate and around the armholes. The top edges of the pauldrons were turned until the gard-

braces were added. Then the turn was added to them. It was called a hautpiece and was the most important turn of all, because it guarded the neck. If a knight's head or neck was struck with a lance, he was usually toppled off his horse.

Small bars were sometimes riveted to the plates to catch the lance and slide it away from a weak spot. They were called stop ribs. The stop ribs were shaped like pieces of railroad track with a hollowed-out side. The lance was caught in the hollow and slid along the rib until it slipped

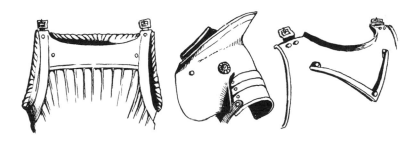

off the plate. A stop rib was riveted to the top of the breastplate to keep the lance away from the neck. Others were added to the pauldrons and the plates of the vambrace and leg harness.

The Germans had their own way of dealing with the problem, as you might expect. They shaped their longer, flatter plates into pointed ridges or keels down the middle. These made the lance slide to the left or the right. These ridges became one of the marks of German armor.

The Germans liked to keep their armor light, so they

did not use as many double plates as the Italians. They made their armor stronger by "rippling" it. That means they hammered long grooves into the plates so that they curved up and down like waves. We use corrugated cardboard and corrugated iron today when we need something stronger than flat sheets.

The grooves or ripples were called flutes. They were used as decoration on Egyptian and Greek columns. This is where the name came from: the rounded grooves looked like the inside of flutes, or tubes, cut down the middle. Flutes also worked like turns or stop ribs. They could catch a lance point and slide it off the plate. They also made a pleasing decoration. Anything that could do three jobs at once was bound to be popular with the thrifty Germans, and fluting became part of the German style like the keels on the plates.

As the plates became bigger, articulated plates became more important so that the knight could keep his freedom of movement. Many of the larger plates were split up into several smaller ones with sliding rivets.

The cuirass was split in two across the middle. The upper parts were still called the breastplate and backplate. The lower parts were called the placket and the lower backplate. The lower plates overlapped the upper ones slightly and were fastened to them by straps and buckles. By the middle of the fifteenth century, the tops were slanted or curved up to a point in the middle which almost reached the neck. They were fastened on with sliding rivets or sliding nuts and bolts. Sometimes they were split across the middle too, especially the backplate, which had to be able to curve more when the knight bent over.

The pauldrons were often divided into several pieces and more lames were used to fasten them to the vambraces. The reinforcing plates on the cuisses often reached up to the hips and were split up into several articulated plates.

At the beginning of the Age of Plate, the Italian armorers had been famous for a century. The German armorers had a long way to go to catch up.

They were determined that no one was going to mistake their work for Italian armor. They began to make armor with straight edges, sharp angles, and box-shaped plates. In fact, the first truly German piece of plate was called a *Kastenbrust*, or box chest. It was a square breastplate which slanted away from the chest down to the bottom of the ribs, then bent back almost at right angles to meet the waist. At first it was worn alone, strapped over the haubergeon. The stick-in-the-mud German knights were not going to give up their mail any quicker than the English knights had given up their long surcoats a century before.

A backplate and fauld were added about 1430. The fauld was made of eight or nine wide lames and came down to the knees. Riding in one looked impossible, but somehow the German knights managed it. They certainly were not getting much help from their armorers. No wonder the Italians were able to sell their armor in Germany.

The German knight now looked as if his top half had been jammed into a steel box after he had been dropped into a small steel tent. Add to this clumsy, shapeless vambraces and leg harness and you have the Kastenbrust suit —the ugliest, most uncomfortable, and least efficient armor ever made.

Even the armorers began to see this. They took another look at Italian armor and began again. Italian curves softened the square lines of the breastplate. It became long and slender and sloped in at the waist. The fauld was shortened. Slimmer vambraces and leg harness were made in the Italian style although the vambrace was still made in three separate pieces and tied to the hauberk sleeves. The German armorers turned the Kastenbrust suit into the greatest armor in the history of armor-making, the Gothic suit.

It is called the Gothic suit because it was like Gothic architecture with its tall, slender lines, pointed curves, and cusped decorations. (Cusps were small points with curved sides.) Gothic armor was the perfect armor: light, strong, comfortable, and graceful. The Italian armorers were soon copying it, even though it was a German idea. They made the best of it, though. Some of the finest Gothic suits came from Italian workshops.

There is a picture of a German Gothic suit on page 193. The cuirass is slimmer than the Italian type and slopes in

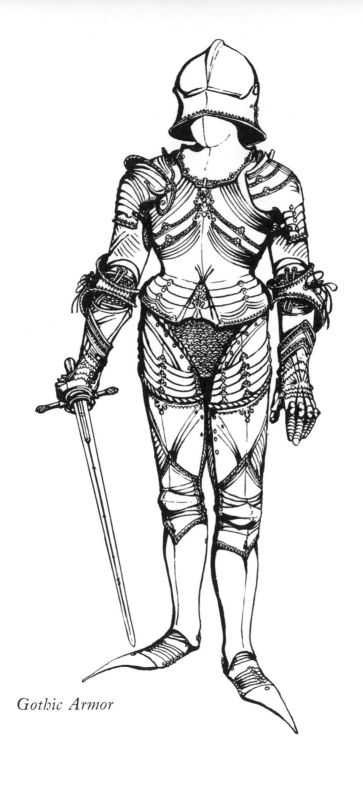

Gothic Armor

to the waist, which is very narrow. The knights were as vain as movie actresses about their waist measurement. You *had* to have a slim waist to get into a Gothic cuirass. The pauldrons are smaller than Italian pauldrons, and the vambraces are fastened together with thongs instead of sliding rivets. The fauld is very short and has no tassets. Instead, the double plate on top of the cuisse comes right up to the hips.

The gracefully shaped leg harness is in the Italian style, but the decoration is German. The top of the cuisses, the couter wing, the lame above and below the knee, and many other plates are decorated with a narrow band of latten cut into rows of fleurs-de-lys. The points of the cuirass plates end in a scrolled design which was popular in Germany. These plates are also cusped along the edge and the cusps are repeated on the fauld, the beaver, the cuisses, and in several other places. Finally, the plates are rippled with flutes in groups of three.

This is one of the greatest Gothic suits. It was made by Lorenz Helmschmied of Augsburg for the Archduke Sigmund of Tyrol.

In Italy, the Gothic style was slightly different. The cuirass was much rounder and was usually made in one piece. The fauld was longer and tassets were usually added to it. The pauldrons were larger and so were the couter- and knee-cop wings. The vambrace was fastened with sliding rivets. A small fringe of mail hung below the bottom lame of the knee cop. The sabatons were often made of mail with a plate heel and toe. (Why the Italians decided to go back to mail sabatons in the fifteenth century is a complete mystery.)

The helmet of Sigmund's suit is one of the new fifteenth-century helmets. It is called a sallet from the German name for it, *Schallern,* which means a shell—what sort of shell no one seems to know. The sallet was very popular in Germany during the fifteenth century. It was a kind of kettle hat. The kettle hat was still being worn but its shape had changed quite a lot. The skullpiece was

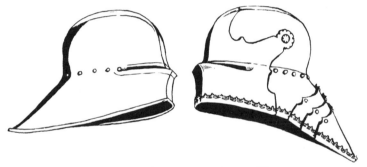

oval like the crown of a derby hat. The brim curved down and a slit was cut in the front of it so that the knight could see where he was going.

The sallet was a kettle hat with the brim going straight down around the front and sides of the head as far as the bottom of the ears, with the sight cut in the front. Sometimes, the front was cut into a curved facehole and covered with a curved visor, pivoted to the sides of the skullpiece. The back of the sallet curved down low over the neck and then stretched out into a long, pointed neckguard. By the end of the fifteenth century, the point had become so long that it had to be made in three articulated pieces so that it would not spike the knight between the shoulder blades when he threw his head back.

The Italian type of sallet was called a barbute. (The name barbute comes from the Italian word *barbuta*, which means bearded. Why the Italians called it a "bearded" helmet is not very clear. It may have been because the

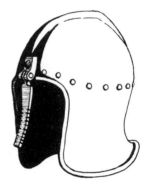

barbute was worn without a beaver or a visor, so the knight's beard would have shown underneath.)

The sides of the barbute curved down to the shoulders but it did not have the long, pointed tail of the German sallet. The crown of the barbute was slightly pointed and had a ridge or keel running from front to back. The face-hole was shaped like a letter T, with the eyeholes as the arms of the T. Sometimes the eyeholes were pointed at the ends. This kind of barbute looked very like the hoplite's Corinthian helmet. It may have been copied deliberately, since Italy had become the home of the new studies of Greek and Roman art which we call the Renaissance. Another type of barbute had a more open facehole shaped like a heart. It was called a celata, which is the Italian way of pronouncing sallet.

The bascinet had disappeared about 1420 because it was too light for fifteenth-century fighting. The great bascinet had replaced it until 1450. Then it became a

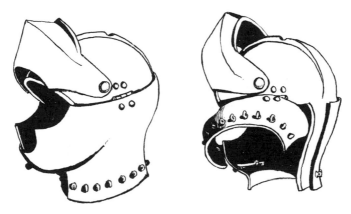

tournament helmet. A new kind of bascinet called the armet came into use after 1420. It had a close-fitting round skullpiece, which was cut off straight above the ears. A narrow strip called a nucquepiece ran down from the back of it. Long, wide cheekpieces were hinged to each side. They ran right round the head. In front, they overlapped and were fastened together with a spring pin. At the back, they met and covered the nucquepiece. The visor had a short, blunt point. It was called a sparrow beak. It was attached to hinged pivots like the pig-face visor.

About 1440, a beaver was added. It covered the bottom half of the visor and the chin and had two or three throat plates attached to the bottom. It was strapped round the neck. To stop the strap from slipping down, a short metal rod was screwed into the nucquepiece below it. A disc or rondel was attached to the end of the rod for decoration, and gave the helmet its name of armet à rondel. A short camail was hung on staples around the bottom of the

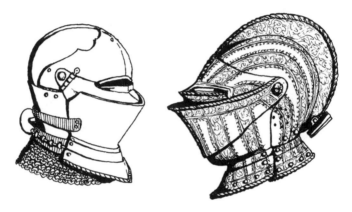

cheekpieces until about 1500, when it was replaced with a gorget.

The armet was usually worn as part of the Maximilian suit, which replaced the Gothic style of armor at the beginning of the sixteenth century. It was named after the German Emperor, Maximilian I. Maximilian was a strange man. Although he lived at the height of the Renaissance, he wanted to turn the clock back to the great days of knighthood and the Crusades. He was interested in everything to do with armor, tournaments, and chivalry. He founded a royal workshop at Innsbruck, where most of the great German armorers worked at one time or another, and he may well have helped to design the Maximilian suit. He certainly spent enough time breathing down his armorers' necks and telling them why his ideas were better than theirs. (We have had one example of that already.)

Maximilian armor is big, burly, and rounded. The light and graceful Gothic armor was not made to stand up to gunfire. Maximilian armor was. The difference between them can easily be seen if you compare the suit shown on page 200 with the Gothic suit on page 193. The cuirass of the Maximilian suit is very short and rounded into a globe. The fauld is very long and the tassets have become a part of it. Like the fauld they are divided into articulated strips. The pauldrons are very large with high hautpieces riveted to them. The vambraces and leg harness are broader and less curved. The couters are enormous, and the wings of the knee cop are the size of saucers. The sabatons end in flat, wide toes. They are called bear-paw sabatons. The gorget is worn underneath the cuirass and helps to carry the weight.

All the plates are made with round, smooth edges and are covered all over with deep, wide flutes. Even the top of the helmet and the visor are fluted. They also have thick rims filed into rope patterns. They are called roped borders. The plates are decorated with fine engraving.

Maximilian armor is marked by its size and roundness,

Maximilian Armor, about 1530

by its deep fluting, and by its fine engraving. It was the last full battle armor worn and was worthy of that honor.

In the last years of the Maximilian period, many suits of armor were made in imitation of the knight's everyday clothes. The imitation even went as far as showing the stitches by punching out the shape of the thread. Some suits were made in imitation of the Greek and Roman "muscled" cuirass. Visors were shaped like human or animal faces. The plates were etched and engraved all over and crusted with gold and jewelry. These were fancy-dress suits, used for parades.

Unfortunately, the fashion for this overdecorated armor became popular. After 1550, it became the style called the Pisan style, after the town of Pisa in Italy where much of it was made. In the Pisan period, the armorer ceased to be a craftsman. He became a goldsmith. He was no longer interested in making battle armor. He used the plates merely to show off his skill as an engraver or sculptor.

The Age of Armor was really finished. The knight was not needed or wanted on the battlefield. He fought for his own fame and glory; the new armies fought to win. They did not want armor, although it hung on until the middle of the sixteenth century. The armorer became a blacksmith once more. He found that it was more profitable to make hundreds of cheap pieces for the king's soldiers, which he could turn out in a few weeks, than to work for months on one suit of armor for a knight, who would probably forget to pay him anyway.

The professional armies were divided into heavy cavalry armed with lances, light cavalry armed with hand guns, arquebusiers and musketeers, and pikemen who protected the gunners while they were reloading.

The heavy cavalry wore three-quarter armor. This was a suit of plate without the leg harness. The tassets were brought down to the knees and the greaves were replaced with long leather riding boots. The light cavalry wore a cuirass and gorget or a mail shirt, with long plate gauntlets to protect their right arms from flashback when they fired their guns. They wore a new kind of open sallet called a burgonet or Burgundian sallet. It had a rounded skull-piece with a curved neckguard and a wide, flat peak called a fall. Large cheekpieces were hinged to the sides and tied under the chin. A high beaver called a buffe was attached to the cheekpieces and the fall with hooks.

The infantry wore a light open helmet called a morion, which is French for the crown of the head. It was the

last of the kettle hats. The skullpiece was round and had a tall, rounded comb. The brim curved up to a point in front and behind like the horns of the moon. Narrow, shield-shaped earpieces, with thongs to tie under the chin, hung on either side. Another kind of morion called a

cabasset was worn in Spain. It had a high skullpiece that looked like one end of a melon. It even had a small, stalk-shaped point on top. The brim was narrow and flat. It was nothing more than the everyday hat of the time, made in steel.

The front rank of pikemen, or armed pikes as they were

called, wore a corselet. This was a roughly made cuirass with a gorget of two plates and wide square tassets. Sometimes a simple vambrace was worn with it. The armed pikes carried a fifteen-foot pike and a sword. The other pikemen, or dry pikes, wore a brigandine or jack with mail sleeves. They were armed with a pike and dagger.

The gunners, who knew better than anyone else that armor was a waste of time, had given it up altogether. They had worn a morion, but by the seventeenth century they had gotten rid of it and wore a long leather coat called a buff and a wide-brimmed hat with a plume.

Officers wore more armor simply to show that they were officers. They had a narrow cuirass which slanted in to the waist. The breastplate was sharply ridged and curled down into a sort of pouch or hump at the bottom. This copied the "peascod" style of tunic or doublet which was worn at the time. Long tassets made of many small plates ran down from the cuirass to the knee. Large, crude pauldrons and straight "drainpipe" vambraces were sometimes added to the cuirass. The helmet worn was usually an armet or a morion.

By the middle of the seventeenth century, only the heavy cavalry wore battle armor. They had a simple burgonet and a cuirass. The burgonet was a round skullcap with a flat fall riveted to the front. Steel bars ran down from the fall to make a faceguard. The neck was protected by a flap of articulated plates riveted to the back of the skullcap. From this the helmet took the name of "lobster-tail" burgonet. The cuirass was made up of a plain waist-length breastplate and backplate with a waist belt and buckles at the shoulder. Armor had become so rare by that time that the heavy cavalry were called cuirassiers after their armor.

Noblemen still wore armor sometimes, but not for fighting. They posed in it when they were having their portraits painted.

It took four thousand years to make the armorer a craftsman, but only 250 years to put him out of business. But in those 250 years he had been perhaps the greatest craftsman of his time. He had certainly come a long way from the armor-making blacksmith.

The thing that helped to make him a craftsman was the water wheel. The water wheel gave him power to drive machinery, and the machines did much of the heavy work. Water-powered stamp mills crushed his iron ore; water-powered bellows heated his furnaces high enough to melt the iron out of it. Water-powered tilt hammers beat the blocks of pure iron into sheets. The armorer did not have to waste time hammering a few small pieces of iron out of the "bloom." He could use the time to design and make better and more beautiful armor.

His tools were still the blacksmith's tools. Besides his forge and bellows, he used hammers and anvils, pincers, chisels, cutters, files, and grindstones.

He had many different kinds of hammers to do dif-

ferent jobs. Sledgehammers called sherrys or flatteners were used to beat the plates roughly into shape. Smaller hammers with specially shaped heads were used to finish them. There were also riveting hammers, and embossing hammers. Most of the small hammers had copper heads so that they would not scratch the metal. There were as many kinds of anvil as there were hammers: large, heavy ones called maids or beckirons (*beak irons*, from the large point at one end) for the rough work, smaller ones called stakes for finishing. The stakes were iron bars with specially shaped tops. They were fitted into holes in the top of the workbench, so the armorer could sit down to his work.

To make a suit of armor, the armorer made a pattern like a dress pattern which fitted his customer exactly. (If the knight was, say, an Englishman who wanted to have his armor made in Italy, he sent along a suit of clothes so that the armorer could get his measurements.) Rough iron sheets from the hammer mill were marked out from the patterns and cut to size with chisels and shears or cutters. They were heated and beaten into rough shape with the sledgehammers. Then they were finished off cold, with special hammers, to make them stronger. Finally rims and turns were added.

The men who shaped the plates were called hammermen. When they had finished, the suit was fastened together. It probably did not fit the first time and had to be reworked several times. When the master armorer was satisfied, the suit went to the millmen, whose job was to file the edges smooth and polish the surfaces on grindstones. (These, too, were driven by water power.) At this point, the decoration was added: latten borders, gilding, etching, or engraving. Finally, the locksmiths, who made the fastenings, added the buckles and hinges and fastening pins.

The whole suit was polished or buffed with white soap, which was also used to grease the axles of the grindstones. The plates were painted or varnished or tinned (like our food cans) to prevent them from rusting. At last, the armor was ready to wear. That is, if the knight paid his bill. Many times the armorer was not paid for his work. An English armorer named William Pickering made a harness for the Prince of Wales and was not paid until two years after the prince's death.

The craft of the armorer can be seen everywhere in his work; in the way in which the plates fitted the man, and were fitted to each other. He could not only curve the plates several different ways to fit the different parts of the knight's body, he could make them graceful at the same time. Using only a hammer, he could make a plate thick where strength was needed, then thin it off toward the right side. In this way, he kept the armor both strong and light. He could shape small lames, like the lames of the gauntlets, so that they moved easily over each other without showing a gap. His skill could not be matched today. He worked without the fine measuring devices used by modern engineers. He worked by "feel," which came from love of his material and pride in his craft.

Perhaps the best example of the armorer's skill is the way he got round the problem of fastening plates together so that the knight was fully protected but could still move freely. We have met some of these fastenings already: straps and buckles, hinges, sliding rivets, turning pins, "umbrella-catch" spring pins, staples and pins and hinged pivots like those used for the pig-face visor. There were still more.

The cheekpieces of the armet were fastened with another kind of spring pin. This was a long stud fastened on one end of a strip of springy steel. The other end of

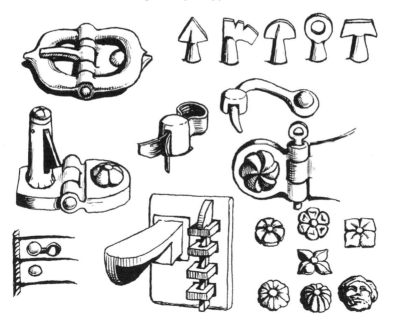

the strip was riveted to the inside of the plate. The stud stuck up through a hole. When another plate was slid across the hole, it pushed the stud down. When it was in place, the stud sprang up again and locked it.

Staples were fastened with split pins called linchpins, or with a small hook which swung on a rivet, something like the catch on a woodshed door or a tool cabinet. A very simple fastening was called the stud-and-keyhole. One plate had a small mushroom-shaped stud at the edge. The plate which was to be fastened to it had a slot shaped like a keyhole. The stud went through the wide part of the "keyhole" and slid down to the bottom, where it caught on the edges of the slot. It was held there by the spring of the plates.

Added to all these, there were sliding bolts, like sliding rivets, wing nuts, and different kinds of screws. And all of them made by hand. It makes quite a list.

The plates were lined with leather, or with padding covered with linen, canvas, or silk, glued or riveted into place. The padding was supposed to be of wool, but sometimes the armorer cheated and used cheap fillings such as dried grass instead. Padded linings made the armor unbearably hot inside, but they had to be used to lessen the shock of blows and to stop the plates from chafing or cutting the knight's skin. Many a knight smothered in his shock-proof helmet because his visor stuck and the vents did not let in enough air.

The armorers learned to decorate their armor in many

Latten Border

Engraved Border

Etched Niello Design

Pierced Design

Embossing

ways. The simplest and sometimes the best way was to add borders of latten or precious metals.

These were often punched or cut into patterns of leaves or fleurs-de-lys. Sometimes the pattern was punched through the plates themselves, especially in the Gothic period. The plates could be colored by dipping them in acids, or "blued," like modern pistols, by passing them through the furnace at a low heat. The most expensive armors were gilded or gold-plated. Cheaper armors were painted. Plain black was very popular in Germany. Elsewhere, much gayer colors and patterns were used. A checkerboard pattern with the knight's badge painted in each square was common. Painting and "blueing" also

Puffed and Slashed Armor, about 1520

helped to stop rusting and to cut down the bright gleam of the steel, which could give away a knight in an ambush.

In the fifteenth century, plates were often engraved. This is done by cutting a design into the steel with a special chisel called a burin. Engraving was hard work, so only the edges of the plate were decorated. At the end of the century, the art of etching was discovered. In etching, the design is cut into the plate with acid. The plate is first covered with a layer of wax and the design is scratched through it. Then the plate is left in a bath of acid until the acid has eaten into the scratched-out areas. The etched lines were often gilded or filled in with a black mixture called niello to bring the design out. Since etching was so much easier than engraving, the whole plate was covered with decoration. Great artists like Dürer and Holbein drew designs for the armorers.

Sometimes plates were covered with brightly colored velvet. Knights' brigandines were always covered with velvet, and the rivet heads were gilded, too. Cloth-covered armor was a favorite in Italy and was used for parade armor everywhere.

Parade armor and Pisan armor were nearly always embossed. In embossing, the plate is pushed out into different shapes from behind with special hammers and punches. Fluting was a kind of embossing, but it was useful. Most embossing was anything but useful. The raised designs stretched the armor thin, and the bumps and creases spoiled the glancing surfaces.

Pisan armor was not only embossed, it was often crusted with gold. This kind of decoration is called damascening after the city of Damascus where it was first used. Cuts were made in the plates with a chisel and gold wire was hammered into them. But, unlike the inlaid steel runes and spells of the Viking swordmakers, which were filed flat, the damascened design was left sticking up above the surface of the plate.

Before the armorer could sell his work, he had to show that it could stand up to punishment. This was called proving the armor. In the early days, armor was proved by taking a swing at it with a sword or mace. In the fifteenth century, a crossbow was used, and finally, in the sixteenth century, an arquebus or musket. If the armor stood up to the test it was called armor of proof. (We still use the word today—bullet-proof vests, shower-proof coats, and so on.) If it did not, it was called "good and sufficient" armor, although it was nothing of the sort. It seems that the armorers, besides everything else, were the first advertising men. When the armor had been proved, the armorer stamped the plates with his mark, just as companies today give guarantees on their goods.

Most noblemen had their own personal armorers, who traveled everywhere with them. The armorers always carried tools to make repairs, spare rivets, oil, cleaning materials, blankets to store the plates in, and so on—a whole workshop, in fact.

In the sixteenth century, three royal workshops were

started: the first at Innsbruck in 1504 by Maximilian, the second in London by Henry VIII in 1515, and the third in 1551 at Aarboga in Sweden by King Gustave Vasa. Maximilian's workshop made many fine suits of armor but the other two were never much good.

Besides the royal workshops, there were the workshops of the great free-lance armorers.

In Italy, the greatest armorers were the Missaglia family. (Their full name was de Negroni da Ello detto Missaglia, but Missaglia will do for us.) They lived in Milan and many generations of Missaglias made armor there. They had immense workshops where they employed many men and turned out thousands of suits of armor. In any armor gallery, you will find a good number of Missaglia suits. After a while, you begin to feel that all the armor made in Italy was made by them. Especially when you discover that another great family of armorers, the Negrolis, was part of the Missaglia family. Their name came from the Negroni part of the Missaglia name. It was changed so that nobody would mix up the two families with each other.

In Germany, the greatest armorers were the Helmschmieds, who also had another name, Colman. The first name was their guild or "working" name, the other was their family name. Not much is known about them, although there were several generations of Helmschmieds who made armor. The best of them all were Lorenz and his brother George, who worked in the second half of the fifteenth century. Many experts think that they are not only the best of the Helmschmieds but the finest of all armorers.

We have the names of many of the other great craftsmen armorers: the Seusenhofers, who ran Maximilian's workshop for over seventy years; Matthew Frauenpriess and Anton Peffenhauser, of the city of Augsburg; Caspar Rieder, the Topf family, and the Treytze family of Innsbruck; the Grosschedel family of Landshut; and Kunz Lochner of Nuremburg. In Italy, there were Pompeo della Chiesi and Lucio Piccinino of Milan, and Bartolemmeo Campi of Pesano. In most cases, we have nothing but their names. Nobody wrote down their life stories or started fan clubs for them.

But they themselves left us something far finer than their life stories—they left us their work.

Words, Words, Words

Many words used to describe the different parts of a plate armor suit are French. In this book, I have always used the English name where there is one. In some cases, however, there are no English words, or we do not know what they were. Many words were spelled in many different ways, too. Each writer on armor has his own pet words. Nineteenth-century writers even made up words when they could not be bothered to find out the proper ones. And there are times when we do not know just what piece of armor the medieval writer is describing. Anyway, here are some of the other words you will come across from time to time.

Helms are often called *heaumes,* which is simply the French spelling. *Sallets* are also spelled *salades* and *salads. Barbutes* are often *barbuts. Kettle hats* are also *chapels-de-fer* or simply *chapels,* which is French for iron hat, or *Eisenhuts,* which is the same thing in German.

There is a lot of argument about whether barbutes, sallets, and armets came from bascinets or from kettle hats, and you will find them in museums sometimes labeled as one and sometimes as the other. It does not really matter a great deal.

Visors are called *visières* (French). This word is some-times used for the sight as well. *Eyehole* and *sight* mean the same thing. *Vents* are also called *breaths*. *Gorget* and *beaver* are often used for one another.

Shoulderpieces are sometimes called *pauldrons* what-ever their size and shape. *Epaulière* (French) is also used for *pauldron*. We have already seen how many different mixed-up ways there are of naming the parts of the vam-brace. To add to them, one twentieth-century writer called *couters elbow cops. Couters* is also written *cowters. Coudière* is the French for *couter*.

Cuirie is sometimes written *quiret* and *curace*. Some-times *plates*, or pairs of plates, is used for *cuirie*, which is wrong.

The *placket* is also called a *pansière*, which is a nine-teenth-century word. The *fauld* is sometimes called a *skirt of taces*, which is a made-up word. (Somebody ob-viously thought that *tassets* meant "small taces.") *Tassets* are called *tuiles*, which is another made-up word from the nineteenth century.

Cuisses are sometimes spelled *cushes* or *quisses. Knee cops* are often called *genouillères*, a made-up French word, or *poleyns. Greaves* is often used by some writers for both *greaves* and *schynbaldes*.

Sabatons are sometimes called *sollerets*.

Mail is called lots of different things. Nineteenth-cen-tury writers thought that the different ways of showing mail in drawings, carvings, and tapestries were actually different kinds of mail. Actually the artists and sculptors were just bored with drawing link after link after link. They used straight lines and different patterns to save time. Anyway, the nineteenth-century writers dreamed up chain mail, banded mail, mascled and rustred mail and trellised armor. Since none of them existed, there is no point in going into what they were all supposed to be.

But, as you can see, we still have a long way to go before our knowledge of armor is complete.

Herald Sounding the Onset

7
The Tournament

Games of war are probably as old as war itself. Men who had to fight in earnest usually liked to fight for fun as well. It was the best way to train men for battle in the days before there were any professional armies.

The Spartans had war games, like a modern army's battle practice. In Roman times, there were the gladiators who fought in armor before huge crowds. Then there was a game called the Ludus Trojae, or Trojan Game, in which young noblemen in light armor gave a riding display in the circus. It was very popular with the Goths when they became the cavalry of the Roman legions. They turned it into a sham battle between two teams of riders.

The Vikings had a dueling game called Holmganga,

which means "going to the island." At first, the duel was fought on a real island in a stream. Later, a blanket was laid down on a flat piece of ground or a square was marked out with posts. The two Holmgangers used swords and shields. They took turns hacking at each other until one of them stepped out of the square. Sometimes, neither one would retreat and they fought to the death. The winner took everything the loser had—including his wife. The Holmganga was really a sport, though sometimes it was used to settle a quarrel. There were professional Holmgangers who fought for profit like our prize-fighters.

The knights' war game was the tournament. Tournaments began about the time that Charles Martel was turning his Frankish infantry into feudal knights. It probably came from the Trojan Game, which had been passed on from the Goths to the Franks. Its name seems to have come from the French word *tourner* or the Latin word *tornare*, both of which mean to turn. This is odd, because in the tournament the idea was to make straight for your man and knock him flat as quickly as possible. The turning may have been some part of the Trojan Game and the name simply hung on into feudal times.

The early tournaments were savage and bloody games. They were no different from real battles except that the fighters were supposed to be friends. They certainly did not act like friends. A group of knights who had nothing else to do would find a flat piece of ground, choose sides, and then hack away at each other until everyone was exhausted or wounded or dead. Sometimes, as many as three thousand knights could be seen having a good time killing each other.

This may seem a strange way of enjoying yourself, but it was the perfect sport for the early feudal knights. They were violent men who did not know what mercy and gentleness were. They had never heard of the Code of Chivalry, which meant so much to the knight in medieval times. When the feudal knight used the word *chivalry*, he meant cavalry. The word came from the French word *cheval*, meaning a horse.

Charles Martel needed violent men to face the Moorish invaders. Later they were needed to push back the barbarian Slavs and Magyars. They saved Europe from the Vikings too. By the tenth century, their job was done. Unfortunately, they did not retire quietly. They never did anything quietly. They were the only trained fighting men in Europe. Mounted on great horses and armored in mail, they could not be beaten. They seized power by force and held it by force. War was not only their job, it was what they liked to do best. Tournaments came a close second to serious fighting.

This made the early knight hard to get along with. It is hard to tell who hated him the most: his king, the Church, or the common people.

The king hated the knights because they were forever making trouble. They fought among themselves, and, when they were not doing that, they plotted against the king. They were hopeless in war. They fought for glory, not to win battles for the king. It was every man for himself, without sense or discipline. Against Vikings and Moors, this did not matter so much. The crushing weight of the heavily armored knights and their reckless courage usually won. But when two armies of knights met, discipline and brains were needed. The knights were short of both. The lucky side won this kind of slugging match, which did not suit the king at all. Since these were the only troops he had, he had to put up with it. But it did not make him love the knights any better. Besides, they hardly ever paid their taxes.

The Church hated the knights because they robbed monasteries, burned convents, killed bishops and priests without mercy, and had no respect for God or His Church. They also had a nasty habit of making clergymen out of their relations. In this way, they could always be sure of a proper blessing for their dirty work.

The commoner hated the knight for many reasons. The knight burned his house, stole his goods, trampled over his crops, and took away his wife and children for slaves. He himself could be tortured and thrown into prison for no reason. Worst of all, there was no one he could turn to for help. The local lord made the rules and ran his own court. In any case, the common people had few enough rights in the feudal world. To them, the knight was a murdering bandit on a horse.

There were no rules for the feudal knight except his own whim. And at first there were no rules for the tournament either. The battlelike fights were called mêlées, which means mix-ups, and there could not have been a better name for them.

Something had to be done to stop the knights from wiping themselves out. So, in the eleventh century, a knight called Geoffroi de Preuilli set down the first rules for the tournament. They helped to make the mêlée more of a sport and less of a bloodbath. However, it was still a dangerous sort of sport. Geoffroi was killed a few years later in a mêlée at Tours. Even in the thirteenth century, when things were much tamer, knights were killed by the hundred every year. In 1250, sixty of them died in a single tournament at Neuss in Germany.

By this time, the tournament was a holiday for everyone. For the noblemen, there was their favorite sport, followed by banquets and dances at the local castle. For the common people it usually meant a day from work, with a fair, street singers, acrobats, and strolling players. The commoners enjoyed watching the fight as much as the noblemen enjoyed taking part in it. The spectators took sides and cheered and booed like a football crowd. They even threw rocks at knights that they did not like. Sometimes the knights lost their tempers with each other —which was always an easy thing for them—and what started out as a pleasant day's sport turned into a free-for-all. Even the audience joined in, hurling stones and slingshots and dragging the knights out of their saddles. Tournaments often ended in riots.

The Church tried to stop the trouble by banning tournaments. This happened three times in the eleventh century alone. A knight who died in a tournament was not allowed Christian burial. But by the time he was ready to be buried the knight was past caring. While he was alive, he could no more give up tourneying than he could give up breathing. Church ban or not, the tournaments went on.

The kings tried to stop them too, but they had no better luck than the Church. They did not like the knights much, but every time a knight was killed they lost a trained soldier—and a taxpayer. Besides, tournaments gave the noblemen a perfect chance to get together and plot. Royal decrees forbidding tournaments came out about once every two years; there were forty-one of them between 1270 and 1350.

Still, the tournament became more and more popular. During the thirteenth century, the knights spent much of their time fighting in tournaments or traveling to or from them. Whenever a tournament was announced, knights would set out from all over Europe. Some of them spent weeks on the road to get there.

The tournament had changed a lot by this time. There was a judge to see that the rules were kept. There were more rules to keep. And, in the middle of the century, a completely new kind of tournament appeared. It was called the joust, from the Latin word *juxtare*, to collide.

The joust was a trial of skill, not a trial of strength. Two knights fought with lances, which were the true knightly weapon. They fought to unhorse one another, not to kill. In any case, the judge could stop the fight at any time and prevent any serious injury being done. The tournament was growing more civilized as it became part of the Code of Chivalry.

The Code of Chivalry was the rule by which the medieval knights lived. At least, it was the mark they were supposed to aim at, though most of them fell far short. Chivalry no longer meant cavalry; it meant behaving like a nobleman.

The feudal knight, as we have seen, was a nuisance to everyone. His way of life was fighting, rioting, and murder: this is what he was trained for. All this fighting spirit had to be turned to something new, if life was to go on. The Church found the answer in the Crusades. Here the knight's love of battle could serve a good purpose. The knights needed a lot of persuading before they agreed to take the cross, but in the end they did. Fighting for God changed the knights' whole way of looking at things. The best examples of what happened are the knightly orders which were founded in the twelfth century. The knights became monks as well as warriors. The three great orders were the Hospitallers, who looked after the sick or wounded who reached the Holy Land; the Teutonic knights, who did the same work but were all Germans;

and the Templars, who protected the pilgrims while they traveled, and guarded the Holy Places.

These knights found that they could do something worthwhile for other people and still be great warriors too. The strict rules of the orders taught them a sense of discipline. The hard way of life of the monk taught them self-control and humility. In other words, the Crusades gave the knights a sense of honor.

Another important part of the Code of Chivalry was courtesy and good manners. Courtesy meant the art of paying court to a lady. The feudal knights had no time for that; they were more interested in their weapons, their horses, and their hawks. Besides, the feudal ladies were as tough as the men. When their husbands went Crusading, the ladies took over the job of defending the castle. But after the Vikings and Saracens had been defeated, the castle became the knight's home as well as his fortress. The women of the castle turned to decorating it and making it more comfortable. Life became more settled. Travelers were taken in and given food and lodging and protection for the night.

Many of these travelers were minstrels and troubadours. They were wandering musicians who sang for their suppers. For the lord of the castle they sang battle songs of the great heroes. (One of the greatest was a knight called Sir Bevis of Hampton. He would not have been a hero today. Before he settled down to the life of a country gentleman, he had slaughtered over six hundred innocent people. This did not seem to bother the knights at all.)

For the ladies, there were love songs in which every woman was a queen or a goddess. The idea was silly and exaggerated, but it caught on. While the knights did not go as far as the troubadours, they did begin to treat women with respect and courtesy. They became ladies' men. They cleaned their fingernails, trimmed their hair, changed their shirts more often, and improved their manners.

Honor, courtesy, respect for God, humbleness, and gentleness made up the Code of Chivalry. By the fourteenth century, all these things had become part of the tournament. This led to the joust's replacing the bloody mêlée.

The joust was the perfect sport for the medieval knight. He fought for the honor of his lady as well as for his own glory. He had a wonderful chance to show off his skill as a warrior and as a horseman out in the open. In the dust and confusion of the mêlée, no one knew what was going on, so no one stood out as a champion. The judge could not see either, and all sorts of dirty work must have gone on. This could not happen so easily in the joust. The knight had to fight honorably whether he wanted to or not. The rules for the joust were strict and the judge was able to enforce them. It was still no sport for weaklings, though.

There were two kinds of joust, the joust à plaisir and the joust à l'outrance.

The joust à plaisir, or joust of peace, was fought for fun. The lances had specially blunted heads called rebated points. The swords had blades made of whalebone. The armor for the joust of peace was made of leather: a cuirie, armplates, and spaudlers. There was a special helm. It was large and round and thickly padded. It had a faceguard of leather and metal strips woven together. Sometimes leather leg harness, called *bainbergs* or leg protectors, was worn too. The armor was all gilded and engraved. The surcoat and ailettes added their bright colors, and the shield was gaily blazoned with the knight's coat-of-arms.

The joust à l'outrance, or joust of war, was a fight with pointed and edged weapons. At first, it was a fight to the death. Later, it came to mean simply a fight with pointed weapons. Even so, many knights were killed. The joust of war was often a grudge fight. Sometimes it was a trial by combat.

When one nobleman was accused of a crime by another, he could choose a trial by combat instead of a legal trial. The idea was that God would show who was right by not allowing the guilty knight to win. The knight and his accuser fought a joust à l'outrance. In the case of a trial by combat, it was always fought to the death and sometimes it took all day. The idea seemed to work sometimes. In the fourteenth century, two men named Panniot and Turquant were accused of murdering the Lady Blanche de Bourbon. Turquant said he had nothing to do with it; Panniot said they had done it together. They fought a trial by combat and Turquant was almost the winner. But just as he was about to deliver the deathblow,

Thirteenth-Century Tournament Armor

a bolt of lightning struck and killed the pair of them. Everyone was satisfied that justice had been done. Usually, however, the answer was not found so easily.

During the thirteenth century, the knights wore their ordinary battle armor for the joust of war. In the second half of the century, this always included the great helm, which was the first piece of special tournament armor. The fact that it was heavy and stuffy did not matter too much in jousting. The knight only had to wear it while he was actually fighting. It gave such good cover to the head that a little discomfort was worth it.

In the fourteenth century, jousting armor became much heavier, though the writers never said in what way. Probably the knights wore the heaviest kind of plate—coats-of-plates, vambraces, leg harness, and so on—even though they stuck to their plain hauberks for war.

From this, it seems that the tournament was no longer just another kind of fighting. It was something special and had to be treated differently. We find this happening on the battlefield, where a champion from one side would ride out in front of the battle line and challenge any knight in the enemy's ranks to joust before the real battle began. Jousting was different from just plain fighting.

A tournament started with a challenge. A group of knights—anywhere from two or three to twenty or more —challenged all comers to joust with them. ("All comers," of course, meant all other knights. Commoners were not allowed to joust.) The date and place of the tournament were set down, and any special rules such as the number of courses, or runs, with the lance and the number of strokes with hand weapons. The types of weapon to be used and the sizes they had to be were also included. The challenge was signed by all the knights, who sometimes chose nicknames for the joust. They often fought, for instance, under the names of King Arthur's knights—Galahad, Lancelot, Gawain, and so on.

Sometimes the challengers would defend a bridge or ford, or a road through a narrow valley. This kind of joust was called a passage-of-arms because the other knights had to get past them. This kind of tournament died out, but the name was kept as another word for the tournament itself.

Usually one of the challengers was the host and the tournament took place at his castle. Heralds were sent out to every town and village for hundreds of miles around to read out the challenge in the market squares. They nailed copies of it to trees near every crossroads. Travelers and troubadours carried the news even farther. Before long, knights were heading for the place where the tournament was to be held.

While all this was going on, the tournament ground was made ready. A flat area, about the size of a football field, was marked out and covered with a thick layer of sand. This softened the knight's fall and gave a firm footing to his horse. Two fences were built around the space about six feet apart. The knights' servants took shelter in the space between the fences during the fighting. (Their job was to run out and steady the knight in his saddle after the lances struck. As armor became heavier, they also helped the knight to his feet when he was unhorsed.) The fences were made too high for a horse to jump. They were called the lists, from an old French word *lice*, which means a boundary. Lists came to mean the whole tournament field. The fences were then called the barriers.

Halfway along the barrier on one side, there was a high, covered grandstand for the judge and noble guests. Opposite this was another high stand for the ladies. One of them was chosen as the Queen of Love and Beauty, who gave the prize to the champion jouster. The common folk crowded around the barriers wherever they could find room. The grandstands and the barriers were hung with tapestries from the castle and with other rich materials. Flags, pennons, and bunting flew from every pole and post. It was a gay and colorful sight.

The challengers, or home team, set up their tents at one end of the lists, near a gate in the barrier. They were called the tenans, which means holders, because they held the field; that is, they defended the lists. The knights who came to joust were called venans, or comers. (We still use these words today, when we say of a sporting champion that he holds the field against all comers.)

The venans set up their tents near a gate at the other end of the lists. As each venans arrived, he sent his coat-of-arms to the judge of the tournament to prove that he was a nobleman, and had the right to joust. Then the heralds nailed it to the barrier. The venans paid them a fee called nail money. The heralds could also keep any armor which fell to the ground during a tournament and sell it back to the knight who had lost it. And when a young knight was fighting his first tourney, he had to give up his helm to them and ransom it back.

When the venans had chosen which one of the tenans he wanted to fight, he sent his squire to the knight's tent. Outside, there were two shields, a wooden one and an iron one. If the squire struck the wooden shield, it was to be a joust of peace; if he struck the iron one, a joust of war. The venans was also supposed to have the choice of weapons, though this had usually been fixed in the challenge. During the fourteenth century, the knights usually ran three courses with the lance and took three strokes with the sword. The number of courses kept going up until, about 1500, the joust was fifteen courses with the lance and any number of sword strokes.

On the day of the tournament, the judge examined all the weapons. He made sure that the lances were the same length and that points were properly blunted. When this had been done, the knights and their ladies, all dressed in their best armor and finest clothes, rode down to the lists in a long, colorful parade. As time went by, the parade became an important part of the tournament. In fact, by the sixteenth century, it had grown into a pageant with floats and musicians and bands. Things became

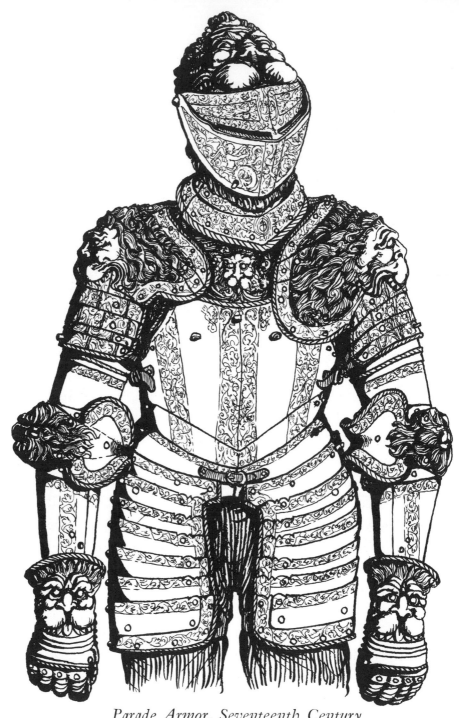

Parade Armor, Seventeenth Century

twisted right around and the jousting became part of the pageant.

When the parade reached the lists, it split up. The knights went to their places behind the barriers at each end of the field. The judge took his seat, and the Queen of Love and Beauty was assisted to her throne. The first two jousters came into the lists and rode to the judge's grandstand, showing off their riding as they went. They saluted the judge and went back to the ends of the lists. The judge gave the signal to begin, the heralds sounded a fanfare on their trumpets, and the two knights lumbered off down the lists to honor and glory and broken bones.

Lumbered is the right word to use. The knight's charger, or *destrier* as it was called, was no prancing steed. It was a great, broad-backed workhorse. The favorite kind of charger was the Percheron, which is used nowadays for the heaviest farmwork. It had the strength to carry the knight and all his armor without tiring, and it gave the knight a solid, steady seat to fight from. Speed was not needed because the knight did not travel very fast in battle. A fast trot was about the best he could manage. A canter or a gallop in full armor would have rattled all the teeth out of his head. If a medieval knight could see a modern movie about knights, where horses charge at racing speed, he would laugh himself sick.

Besides the joust on horseback, there were foot fights. These were more dangerous than the joust. The knights fought with all the ordinary weapons and wrestled too. They used a kind of jujitsu to throw their opponent to the ground or to pin his weapon. Anything was allowed but punching. Punching was frowned on because it was a woman's way of fighting.

On the next to last day of the tournament, the knights took a vacation from fighting to choose sides for a mêlée. The mêlée always took place on the last day and brought the tournament to a close.

After each day's jousting there was a banquet at the castle, followed by dancing and entertainment. Troubadours sang of the day's deeds and there were tumblers, clowns, and dancing bears. While the knights relaxed, the armorers worked to hammer out the dents and replace the broken links so that the knights would be ready again next morning.

Tournaments often went on for weeks. Holding a tournament cost a lot of money. Not only were there the lists to prepare, but all the knights and their ladies had to be fed. Then there were the prizes, which were often very expensive. For the champion, there was a crown of gold laurel leaves. Others who performed well were given jeweled brooches, great silver bowls, chargers with all their harness, suits of armor, hunting hawks, and even, on one occasion, a live bear.

Most of the knights fought for glory, but the prizes were worth winning too. In fact, there were professional jousters, who went from tournament to tournament. Besides the prizes, there was an even more important way to make money. The loser of a joust had to give up his horse and armor to the winner. He usually ransomed them back for a price of five hundred crowns. One way and another, a skillful fighter could make a decent living by jousting.

When the tournament was over, the knights headed for home to talk over what had happened and to wait for the next challenge to arrive.

These were the great days of the tournament. The knights jousted whenever they were given the chance. Everything the knight was trained for and everything he believed in were summed up in this strange sport. His training began when he was seven years old. He was sent away to become a page in another knight's household. There he learned that a knight had to be humble. He did all the small, mean jobs around the castle. He was also taught the religious virtues as well as the knightly virtues. He began to practice with toy weapons and learned to arm his lord.

At fourteen, he became a squire. He learned a whole new set of rules, from fighting beside his master down to keeping his fingernails clean. He learned to play musical instruments, to sing, to dance, and to play chess and back-gammon for the entertainment of his master and the ladies of the household. He learned to wait at table, and to attend to the knight in peace and in war.

Most important of all, he learned how to handle the

great destrier and to fight with lance and sword. He learned to joust at the quintain and run at the ring. The quintain was a man-sized dummy, mounted on a pole. It was fixed on a pivot so that it swung around freely. On one side was a bar with a bag of sand or a bucket of water attached to the end. Unless the lance hit the dummy right in the middle, it swung round and caught the squire on the back with the bag or the bucket. Running at the ring needed greater skill. The small brass ring was hung from a high pole. The squire had to catch the ring on the point of his lance and carry it away.

At twenty-one, the squire was ready for knighthood. The ceremony was called the accolade. It was a solemn occasion. On the night before, the squire was bathed. Like everything else in the ceremony, this had a special meaning. It showed that he intended to start his life as a knight with a pure heart. After the bath, he put on a white tunic (for innocence), a red robe (for self-sacrifice), and a black doublet (to remind him of death). He fasted all night, kneeling in the chapel before his armor and weapons, which were piled upon the altar.

In the morning, he heard Mass and had his sword blessed by the priest. Then he took his knightly vows—to fear God, obey the Church, and serve the king; to live for honor and not for money; to protect the weak and respect women; to be chivalrous, generous, and truthful; to fight for the good of all, never refuse a challenge, and never show his back to the enemy.

Then his armor was put on, his sword was buckled round his waist, and his gold spurs were fastened to his heels. He received the accolade, which means a blow on the neck. It was to remind him that his life was to be one of blows given and taken. It was no love tap: it usually sent him sprawling. Finally, his helm was put on and he leaped, fully armored, into his saddle and showed off his paces as a knight.

By the fifteenth century, the knight's world was dying and the tournament died with it. The new professional soldiers did not fight for fun, and the new merchant-noblemen did not fight at all if they could help it.

The joust became a sport, no more dangerous than mountain climbing. A new safety device was invented. It was called the tilt. The tilt was a barrier down the middle of the lists which kept the knights from running into each other. This often happened in the open lists because the horses as well as the men were too eager to get into the fight.

The tilt started off as a cloth or *toile* (from which the word *tilt* comes) hung over a rope. Before long, it was replaced by a stout wooden barrier, also called the tilt. It was about as high as the knight's waist when he was on horseback. It was the tilt that led the knights to couch their lances across their horse's neck. We have seen how this changed battle armor. It did the same thing to tournament armor. In fact, the knight became so loaded with armor that he could not move.

The helm was a heavier kind of great helm. The sides curved in toward the bottom. The top became flat and slanted down over the eyes to make a pointed peak. The plate over the face was given a sharp keel and curved up higher than the peak. It was designed to protect the knight's face from the stump of his opponent's lance. The sight was a gap between the front plate and the peak. Because of the high front plate, the knight could only see out of it when he bent over his lance. This sight looked like a big, grinning mouth and gave the helm its name of frog-mouth helm. The frog-mouth helm was used until the tournament died out.

About 1450, the great bascinet was added to the tournament armor. Like the great helm, it became bigger and heavier. However, except for a more rounded skullpiece, it kept the same design until the end.

Tilting armor was really a heavy kind of war armor and followed the fashions of war armor. The big difference between them was the size and weight of the double plates and special plates which were added for tilting.

The left hand and forearm were covered by a heavy gauntlet called a manifer, or iron hand. This was a single steel plate which ran from the tip of the fingers to the elbow and fastened to the guard of the vambrace. The lower vambrace on the right arm was also a special tilting piece. It was called a polder mitten. The inside plate bent up at the elbow and became a large, shell-shaped piece.

Sixteenth-Century
Jousting Armor

This curved round the inside of the elbow, and stuck out in a large wing on the outside. It completely covered the upper vambrace as well. Large round besagews were tied to the front of the shoulders. The right one had to be cut away at the bottom so that the lance could go under the arm.

The vamplate of the lance became bigger and heavier. The shield came back into use. The tilting shield was made of wood covered with a thick layer of horn. It was tied to a breastplate with a heavy cord and covered the left side from the shoulder to the waist. The front of the saddle was covered with steel plates. On each side of the saddle was hung a wide, curved plate called a tilting cuisse, which fitted the thigh and knee. Leg harness was not needed in tilting since the lance could not reach the legs over the barrier. The tilting cuisses were there because the fifteenth-century knight liked to play safe.

As the century went by, more and more armor was added until the knight became a mountain of steel. A special breastplate was developed. It was very thick and heavy and bulged out like the nose of a shark in the middle. A special lanceholder called the *queue* was added. This was a long, flat bar, bolted to the side of the breastplate. It ran back under the arm alongside the butt of the lance. The end curled over the butt to hold it steady. The lance rest held up the front of the lance and saved the knight the trouble of holding it for himself. Even so, the polder mitten was screwed to the upper vambrace so that the arm was held fixed in the couching position.

A large double plate called the grandguard was bolted to the left side of the breastplate. It covered most of the breastplate, the upper part of the left arm, and the left shoulder. A double beaver was riveted to the top, and ran up to cover the throat and the bottom of the face.

A heavy placket was added to the bottom of the breastplate. Long laminated tassets were attached to the bottom and ran down to the knees. The ordinary guard of the vambrace was replaced by a much larger one called the pasguard. The bottom of the pasguard curved around the lower vambrace. The square upper part was bent at right angles to it and covered the upper vambrace, the pauldron, and the left side of the breastplate.

On top of everything went a bigger, heavier shield. It was a large rectangle of steel covered with leather. It ran from the neck to the waist and then curved out to cover the lower part of the left arm. The top curved up into a sort of cup. This went round the chin like another beaver (which made three). Sometimes the shield was not covered with leather, but a crisscross pattern of stop ribs was riveted across the front. This was to make sure that the other knight's lance caught and splintered properly. After four thousand years of making glancing surfaces, the armorer was now expected to make un-glancing surfaces.

By the time the knight had been screwed and bolted and pinned and hooked into this outfit, he could scarcely move. He was hardly needed anyway. The tilting suit almost fought the joust by itself.

The tournament became a harmless sort of game, and a silly game at that. All sorts of new types of jousts were invented. By the end of the sixteenth century, there were over forty kinds of jousts and fifteen kinds of foot fights. (The tilt had even been added to the foot fight.) The knights had become more interested in inventing jousts than in fighting them.

Some of the new jousts were very silly. In Germany, there was the mechanical joust. The breastplates and shields for this were made up of several pieces, fastened down over a spring. When a hit was made, they were flung into the air in a shower of metal. Even mechanical horses were used instead of chargers.

Another silly idea was the Hohenzeugstech or high-saddle joust. In this, the saddle was built up so high that the knight was actually standing in his stirrups. The front of the saddle was covered with a large wooden shield. A pair of bars ran back from the shield, one on each side, and pinned the knight's thighs to the saddle. The only danger to the rider was a pair of broken thighs if he swayed back too far.

The tournament was no longer a kind of battle. The mêlée disappeared completely. The aim now was to break lances, for which points were given. The champion was the man who scored the most points. Since the lances had to be splintered, not just snapped off clean, they were made of soft wood and the shafts were hollowed out. Even with all this help, the knights were losing their skill. The number of hits became fewer and fewer. At a tournament called the Tournament of Charlemagne's Tree, held in 1443, only 43 hits were made in 143 courses.

Tilting was really the end of the tournament. Where there was no danger, there could be no glory. And where there was no glory, there was no point in going to all the trouble of a tournament.

By the sixteenth century, the tournament was dead. To entertain themselves, the sixteenth-century noblemen put on pageants and musical plays. Jousting was included in the pageant, but it was only a small part of the show. By this time, in any case, the knights no longer fought each other. They ran courses at a quintain or played running at the ring. In France and Italy, the last sad remains of the tournament was a game called the carrousel. Teams of horsemen threw hollow clay balls at each other and then rode round and round the arena, giving a display of horsemanship. (This is where our fairground carrousel comes from.)

The Age of Chivalry was gone, the Age of the Knight was over. Strangely enough, it was a nineteenth-century poet, Samuel Taylor Coleridge, who wrote the knight's epitaph:

> The knight's bones are dust,
> And his good sword rust:
> His soul is with the saints, I trust.

M-48 General Patton Tank

8

The New Age of Armor

The First Age of Armor ended in the sixteenth century. It seemed then as though armor would never be needed again. For several centuries this was true.

Yet, in our times, armor has returned to the battlefield. The First World War saw men charging across No Man's Land in kettle hats—the familiar "tin hats." These have become a regular part of the modern soldier's equipment. In the same war, German sappers wore steel breastplates as they tunneled their mines into the mud. German machine gunners were protected by steel plates, too, because they had to stay out in the open.

In the Second World War, armor was used more widely still. Airmen began to wear it as well as soldiers. Gunners in the great bombers wore a canvas "flak suit."

This was a tunic, lined with steel plates. Sometimes a placket with a rounded bottom was attached to it by snaps.

During the fighting in Korea, more armor was added to the soldier's equipment—bullet-proof jackets and shorts. They were made of nylon, padded with Fiberglas and lined with specially treated aluminum plates. They were worn to protect the men from hand grenades. Their materials are twentieth century, but their design is medieval. They are nothing more than a coat-of-plates and cuisses.

Even the Space Age is looking back to the time of the craftsmen armorers for ideas. Before long we will be landing men on the moon and the other planets. They will need armor, not against arrows and swords, but against radiation and meteorites. Experts are studying armor to see what they can learn from the men who solved the same problems five hundred years ago.

Perhaps the best armor we have produced is the modern tank. It seems to be the answer that the sixteenth-century armorers could not find: how to make a bullet-proof covering that will still allow the wearer to move. I wonder what Lorenz Helmschmied would say if he could see a forty-ton M-48 General Patton tank, with seven inches of armor, roaring into battle at twenty-two miles per hour. Perhaps he would not be impressed. After all, when he made armor, he made all of it by himself with nothing but his hammers and his hands.

Index

Index

Aarboga armory, 215
accolade ceremony, 240–41
Achaeans, 32, 33, 35
Agincourt, Battle of, 133
Ahmose, of Egypt, 12
ailettes, 141–42, 150, 153, 230
Akkad, archers of, 6
Alfred the Great, 111
anelace, 148
Anglo-Saxons, 99, 110–11, 113
aquilifer, Roman, 58, 59
arbalest, *see* crossbow
archers, 94, 97, 108, 111, 113
   ancient, 2–3, 9, 12, 15–16,
     21, 23, 25–26
   English, 128, 130–36, 158
   see also bows
arm, protection for, 138, 230
   see also couters; vambrace
armets, 197–98, 204, 209–10

armets (*cont.*)
   à rondel, 198
   the name, 217
armies:
   ancient, 2, 4–6, 8–17, 19–28,
     30
   feudal, 101, 109, 111, 133–34
   Greek, 35, 40, 44–47
   mercenary, 134, 172–73
   professional, 2, 172–74, 181,
     201–204
   Roman, 53–62, 95–97
arming coif, 121–22, 127
armor:
   ancient, 2–3, 13–14, 17
   typical, 113–17, 119–27
Armor, Ages of, 171–74, 181–
   82, 201–205, 208, 248–50
   and Age of Mail, 103–105
   Mixed, 129–30, 137–38

armorers, 27, 28–29, 103, 137, 158–60, 163, 181–83, 205–16
  workshops of, 206, 214–16
armor of proof, 215
arquebus, 180–81
arrow, longbow, 131
articulated plates, 158–63, 186, 190–91, 204–205, 209
Assyrians, 2, 18–31
Athenian helmet, 43, 62, 70, 72, 73
Athenians, 34, 47
auxilia, 61, 94, 96–97
axes, *see* battle-axes

backplates, 41–42, 90–92, 139, 168–69, 190–91, 205
Bacon, Roger, 174
badges:
  knights', 124
  Norman, 117
  Roman, 76
  see also coat-of-arms
bainbergs, 230
barbutes, 196–97, 217
barleycorn mail, 114–15
barrel helms, 121–22
bascinets, 126, 127, 156–58, 163–65, 197–98, 217, 242
battering rams, 27–28, 85
battle-axes, 27, 100–101, 108, 111, 149, 184
Bayeux Tapestry, 118
beavers, 166, 198, 202, 245
  the name, 218
bec de fauchon, 149

belts, 39, 42, 47, 93–94
  see also cingulum militari; sword belts
besagews, 153, 244
Bevis of Hampton, Sir, 228
bivalve helmet, 63
Black Prince, the, 144
blazons, *see* coat-of-arms
body armor, 14, 17, 23–24, 39, 41, 47, 64–66, 69–70, 154
  modern, 249–50
  see also cuirass; lorica; thorax
Boeotian shields, 36–37, 40
bombards, 175–76
bowmen, *see* archers
bows, 35, 36, 61, 108
  catapult, 61, 84–85, 134
  composite, 2–3, 12, 15, 21, 26, 27
  see also crossbow; longbow
brassarts, 138
breastplates, 41–42, 90–92, 139, 150, 155, 167, 185, 188–92ff
  modern, 249–50
  tournament, 230, 244–46
brigandine, 167–68, 213
Britons, 110
bronze, use of, 12, 48
buffe, 202
burgonet, 202, 204
byrnies, 106, 111

cabasset, 203
Caesar, Augustus, 77
Caesar, Julius, 61, 72, 77

caltrop, 145
camail, 142, 156–57, 164–66
Camillus, Marcus Furius, 55, 68–69, 72
Campi, Bartolemeo, 216
cannons, 175–79
cap-of-mail, *see* camail
Caracalla, Emperor, 61, 95
carroballista, 84–85
carrousel, game of, 247
catapults, 61, 84–85, 134
cavalry, 43–44
    Assyrian, 26, 27
    professional, 202, 204–205
    Roman, 53, 61, 93, 95–97
Cavalry, Ages of, 6–9, 101
celata, helmet, 197
Celts, 71–72
centurions, 55, 58, 60, 72, 78, 79, 82–83
Chalybes, ironsmiths, 20
chariot, 1–2, 3, 4–9, 12–13, 21–23
Charlemagne, Emperor, 102–104, 109
Charlemagne's Tree, Tournament of, 247
Charles V, king of France, 179
Charles Martel, king of Franks, 100, 101–102, 222–23
Charles the Simple, 109
chausses, 122, 127
Chiesi, Pompeo della, 216
Chivalry, Age of, 247
    Code of, 223, 227–29
Church, and the knights, 223–24, 226, 227

cingulum militari, 93–94
clipeus, Roman, 62
Clovis, 100
clubbing weapons, 27, 118–19, 148–49, 184
coat-of-arms, 124–25, 141–42, 154
coat-of-plates, 155–56, 166–69
cohort, Roman, 58, 60, 84
coif, 105, 113–14, 119
    arming, 121–22, 127
    separate, *see* camails
condottieri, 172
conical helmets, 105, 106, 111, 113, 120
consul, Roman, 54, 88
Corinthian helmets, 38, 42–43, 62, 64, 196–97
corslets, 204
couched lances, 117–18, 120, 241
Courtrai, Battle of, 173
couters, 140–41, 152–53, 160, 163, 186, 188, 194, 199
    the name, 218
crossbow, 129, 134–37, 184
Crusaders, 116, 123, 124, 126, 134, 171–72, 227–28
cuirass, 139, 150, 167–69, 187, 190, 192–94, 199, 202, 204–205
    Roman, 72, 87–89, 90
cuirassiers, 205
cuirie, 139, 218
    see also breastplates
cuisses, 140, 150, 152, 218
    in Korean War, 250

cuisses (*cont.*)
  plate, 161, 188, 191, 194
  tilting, 244

daggers, 148, 184
damascening, 214
Dark Ages, 97, 99–100
darts, Roman, 96
decorations, armor, 66, 87–89,
  153–54, 201, 208, 210–14

Egyptians, 2, 8, 10–18, 19, 31
elbow cops, *see* couters
embossed armor, 213–14
England, 110–13, 130–34, 173
  armor fashions of, 154, 183
épée de guerre, 146
Ericsson, Leif, 106
estoc, 147–48
etching, of armor, 213
Etruscans, 51, 52–53, 55, 62

faceguards, 106, 120–21, 124,
  141, 230, 242
falchion, 147, 184
fashion, and armor, 182–83
fastenings, armor, 209–210
  see also articulated plates
fauld, 169, 186, 191–92, 194,
  199, 216
feudalism, 101, 171, 223–28
field guns, 179
fire pot, 175
flail, military, 149
flak suits, 249–50
fluted armor, 190, 194, 199,
  201, 213
foot fights, 237–38, 246

foot protection, *see* sabatons
foot soldiers, *see* infantry
France, 102–106, 109–10, 133,
  136, 173, 183
francisca, 100
Franks, the, 98, 99–106, 222
Frauenpriess, Matthew, 216
"free companies," 172
frog-mouth helm, 242
fustian, 126–27

gambeson, 116
gardbrace, 187–88
Gauls, 52, 55, 58, 61, 68, 69, 72,
  76, 85, 97, 100
gauntlets, 142, 150, 163, 202
  tournament, 242
Genoa, crossbowmen from,
  134
gens d'armes (gendarmes),
  173
German tribes, 58, 72, 76
Germany, 100, 102, 173, 246
  armorers of, 182–83, 189–95,
  198–201, 211, 215–16
gladiators, Roman, 221
glancing surfaces, 28, 188
gorget, 157–58, 166, 187, 199,
  202, 204, 217
Gothic armor, 182, 192–95,
  198, 199, 211
Gothic tribes, 99–100, 221–22
grandguard, 245
greaves, 39, 42, 48, 62, 76, 87,
  150, 161, 202, 218
Greeks, 31, 32–49, 51
Grosschedel family, 216
gunners, professional, 204

gunpowder, 4, 174–75, 177–78
guns, 174–81, 184
Gustave Vasa, King of Sweden, 215

hacketons, 115–16, 127, 156
Hagenau helmet, 86–87
halberds, 158, 174
hals-berge, 102, 105
hammers:
    armorer's, 205, 207
    war, 149, 184
Harold II, of England, 111, 113
hasta, 67
Hastings, Battle of, 111, 113, 118
haubergeon, 156, 166
hauberk, 105, 113–16, 119–20, 127, 142, 150, 156, 166
hautpiece, 189, 199
helmets, 217
    ancient, 6, 9–10, 14, 17, 23, 24, 26
    Greek, 38–39, 42–43, 48
    of knights, 101, 102, 104–105, 113, 120–22, 125–26, 156–58, 163–65, 188, 195–98, 199
    professional army, 202–204
    Roman, 62–64, 68, 70–71, 72–75, 86–87, 95, 97
helms, 121–22, 125–26, 127, 142–43, 150, 217
    tournament, 156, 230, 232, 242
Helmschmied, Lorenz, 194, 215

Helmschmied family, 215–16
Henry VIII, of England, 215
heraldry, 125
heralds, 124, 220, 235, 237
Hispanic sword, 71–72, 96
Hittites, xii, 1–2, 6–10, 17–18, 19, 20
holmganga, 221–22
hoplites, 40–43, 46, 48, 53, 62
horses, 5, 6–7, 125, 237
Hospitallers, 227
Hundsgugel bascinet, 165
Hurrians, 6–7, 11
Hyksos, 11–12, 13, 16

Iliad, 33, 35, 37
infantry, 100, 110, 111, 158, 168, 202–204
    ancient, 9–10, 12, 15–17
    Greek, 40–43, 46, 48
    Roman, 53, 61, 93–95, 96
Infantry, Ages of, 3–6, 31
Innocent II, Pope, 134
Innsbruck armorers, 146, 199, 215
iron, use of, 2, 20–21, 28
Italian vambrace, 160–61
Italy, 51–52, 134
    armorers of, 170, 182–83, 185–89, 191–92, 194, 196–97, 201, 213, 215, 216

jack, 168
James II, of Scotland, 175–76
javelins, 67–68, 69, 76–77, 96, 100–101
jointed plates, *see* articulated

joust, 226–27, 229–39, 241–47
jupons, 154–55, 166, 169

Kastenbrust suit, 191–92
kettle hats, 126, 150, 158, 195–
    97, 202–203, 217, 249
knee cops, 139–40, 141, 150,
    161, 163, 186, 188, 199
    the name, 218
knights, 98, 101–105, 112–13
    armor of, 113–17, 119–27,
        133, 137–45, 150–58, 160–
        69, 182–201
    end of age of, 171–74, 178–
        79, 181, 201, 205, 247
    and tournaments, 222–47
    training of, 239–41
    weapons of, 100, 102, 117–
        20, 145–49, 184–85
Korean War, armor in, 250

lames, articulated, 160, 161,
    185, 187, 191, 194
lancers, Assyrian, 27
lances, 102, 117–18, 120, 148,
    184, 185
    tournament, 229–30, 244,
        246–47
legionary, 50, 54, 57, 60–76,
    85–97
    life of, 78–85
legions, Roman, 54, 55–62
legs, protection for, 116, 119,
    122, 127, 140, 150, 166,
    230
    see also greaves; knee cops;
        schynbaldes

lists, tournament, 233–37
Lochner, Kunz, 216
London, armorers of, 215
longbow, 128, 129, 130–33,
    136, 137, 184
loricas, 70, 75, 89–93, 95, 97
Ludus Trojae, 221, 222

maces, 27, 118–19, 149, 184
machaira sword, 43–44
Mail, Age of, 103–27, 129
    vs. the bow, 133, 137
    kinds of, 114–15, 218–19
    and Mixed Armor, 129–30
mail tunics, 104–106, 113–15
    see also loricas
maniples, 55–57, 58
Marius, Gaius, 57–58, 60, 61,
    76, 81
matchlock, 180
Maximilian I, Emperor, 183,
    198–99, 215, 216
Maximilian armor, 183, 198–
    201
mêlée, 238, 246
men-at-arms, 173
mercenary troops, 134, 172–73
metals, ancient use of, 2, 28–29
Milanese armor, 170, 215
military flail, 149
minstrels, 228–29
Missaglia family, 215
mitra, Greek, 39, 42, 47
Moors, 101–102, 223, 224
Morgenstern, 149
morion, 202–203, 204
muskets, 181

nasals, 105, 106, 113, 120, 157, 164
neck protection, 73–74, 86, 102, 105
  see also coif; helmets
Negrolis family, 215
Normandy, 109–10
Normans, 109–10, 111–13, 118
Nubian archers, 15

padded linings, 210
parade armor, 213, 235, 236
passage-of-arms, 233
Patton tank, 248, 250
pauldrons, 185–86, 187–88, 191, 194, 199, 204, 245
  the name, 218
paunce, *see* fauld
pavises, 158
pectorals, Roman, 64–66, 70
Peffenhauser, Anton, 216
phalanx, 1, 3–6, 15, 44, 53, 54, 55
Phrygian helmet, 70–71, 72, 87
Piccinino, Lucio, 216
Pickering, William, 208
pig-faced visors, 164–65, 197
pikemen, 203–204
pilum, 67–68, 69, 76–77, 96
Pisan armor, 183, 201, 213–14
placket, 218, 245, 250
plastron, 139
plate armor suits, 181–216
  fashions in, 182–83, 192–205
  making of, 207–14

plate armor suits (*cont.*)
  and Mixed Armor, 129–30, 133, 137, 139, 150–69
  parts of, 137–38, 217–19
polder mitten, 242, 244
pole weapons, 158, 184
poleyns, *see* knee cops
pot helms, 121–22, 125–26, 127, 142–43
Praetorian Guard, 76, 93, 94
Preuilli, Geoffroi de, 225
prickspurs, 144
professional soldiers, *see* armies, professional
puffed and slashed armor, 183, 212

queue, lanceholder, 244
quincunx, Roman, 56–57, 60
quintain, 240, 247

Rameses II, 17–18
rerebrace, 138
Richard the Lion-Hearted, 134
Rieder, Caspar, 216
ring armor, 69–70, 75, 89, 102, 114
Romans, 49, 50–97, 221
  armor of, 29, 62–76, 85–97
rowel spurs, 145

sabatons, 152, 163, 183, 194–95, 199, 218
sallets, 195–97, 202, 217
scabbards, 118, 120, 147
scale armor, 13–14, 47, 69–70, 75, 89, 95, 97, 102, 114

schynbaldes, 140, 150
scramasax, 147
scutum, 66–67, 69, 75–76, 93, 95
seax, 110
serpentine, 180
Servius Tullius, 53, 54
Seusenhofer family, 183, 216
Sherden swordsmen, 15, 16, 17
shields:
    in Age of Mail, 100, 102, 106–108, 110, 111, 113, 116–17
    ancient, 6, 10, 11, 16, 26
    for bowmen, 158
    Greek, 36–37, 39, 40–41, 44
    Roman, 62, 66–67, 69, 75–76, 93, 95
    tournament, 185, 230, 244, 245, 246
shoulderpieces, 47, 69, 87–89, 92, 94, 153, 160, 218
    see also pauldrons; spaudlers
sight, 120, 242
skullcaps, 85, 121–22, 143, 150
    see also bascinets
slashed armor, 183, 212
sollerets, *see* sabatons
Space Age, armor for, 250
Spartan helmet, 43
Spartans, 34, 43, 44–47, 221
spatha sword, 96
spaudlers, 153, 160, 230
spearmen, 16, 27, 40–43
spears, 35–36, 43, 67, 110–11
    see also lances
spiculum, 96

spurs, 144–45
standard-bearer, 58, 59
steel, discovery of, 20
stop ribs, 189, 245
Sumerians, 1, 3–6, 19
surcoats, 122–25, 127, 154–55, 166, 169, 230
    for horses, 125
Swiss infantry, 173–74
sword belts, 71, 94, 118, 120, 127, 147, 184
swordmakers, 108, 146–47
swords, 21, 23, 27, 35–36, 43–44, 71–72, 96
    of knights, 102, 108–109, 117–18, 120, 145–48, 184, 230
Syria, 7, 10, 12, 18, 19

tanks, 248, 250
tassets, 186, 194, 199, 202, 204, 218, 245
Templars, 228
Teutonic knights, 227
thigh defenses, *see* cuisses
thorax, 41–42, 47, 48, 62
throat guards, *see* beavers; gorget
tilt, the, 241–48
tilting cuisses, 244
tippets, 158
Topf family, 216
tournaments, 220–47
trapper, horse's, 125
Treytze family, 216
trial by combat, 230

tribunes, Roman, 54
Trojan Game, 221, 222
troubadours, 228–29
Troy, siege of, 33, 35
tunics, 23–26, 115–16, 155–56
  see also lorica; mail; scale
turning pin, 161, 163, 187

underwear, knight's, 126–27

vambrace, 138, 152–53, 154,
  188, 192, 194, 199, 204
  articulated, 160–61, 163
  tournament, 242–44, 245
vamplate, 148, 244
velites, Roman, 56, 61
ventail, hauberk, 119, 127
vents, 120, 218
vericulum, 96
verutum, 67
Vikings, 99, 105–109, 111, 214,
  221–22, 223, 224, 228
visors, 86, 157, 164–65, 195,
  198, 201, 218
vitis, centurion's, 55

volleys, firing in, 15, 26

war, and history, 1
  as professional, 172–74
  and the Romans, 51–52
war crown, 14
war games, 221–23
war hammer, 149, 184
weapons, 174–81, 202, 204
  ancient, 6, 10, 11, 12, 20, 26–
  27
  Greek, 35–36, 47–48
  of knights, 100, 102, 117–20,
  145–49, 184–85
  Roman, 52, 61, 62, 67–69,
  71–72, 76–77, 84–85, 96
  tournament, 229–30, 233,
  235, 246–47
William the Conqueror, 111,
  113
World Wars, 249–50

yew, for longbows, 130–31

zoster, Greek, 42, 47

About the Author

Sean Morrison has been—in his own words—"puttering around" the subject of armor since he was a boy in England. He was born in Liverpool and received both a B.A. with honors in English and an M.A. from St. John's College, Cambridge.

Mr. Morrison lives in New York City with his wife and three children.

399
M
Morrison, Sean
Armor

Date Due

Moving westward from Assyrians, first to make weapons and armor of iron, this account traces evolution of armor and resulting changes in warfare.